The Narrative Writing Toolkit

In order for students to write effective narratives, they need to read good narratives. In this practical book, you'll find out how to use mentor texts to make narrative writing instruction more meaningful, authentic, and successful. Author Sean Ruday demonstrates how you can teach elementary and middle-school students to analyze the qualities of effective narratives and then help them think of those qualities as tools to improve their own writing. You'll learn how to:

- Introduce your students to the key features of a successful narrative, such as engaging the reader, organizing an event sequence, and crafting a strong conclusion.
- Assess students' writing by evaluating the specific attributes of an effective narrative.
- Make narrative writing an interactive, student-driven exercise in which students pursue their own writing projects.
- Use mentor texts to help students learn the core concepts of narrative writing and apply those skills across the curriculum.
- Encourage students to incorporate technology and multimedia as they craft their narratives.

The book is filled with examples and templates you can bring back to the classroom immediately, as well as an annotated bibliography with mentor text suggestions and links to the Common Core. You'll also find a study guide that will help you to use this book for professional development with colleagues.

Bonus: Blank templates of the handouts are available as printable eResources on our website (www.routledge.com/9781138101531).

Sean Ruday is Assistant Professor of English Education at Longwood University. He is also the author of *The Argument Writing Toolkit, The Informational Writing Toolkit, The Common Core Grammar Toolkit, Grades 6–8,* and *The Common Core Grammar Toolkit, Grades 3–5*.

Other Toolkit Books Available from Sean Ruday
(www.routledge.com/eyeoneducation)

The Argument Writing Toolkit
Using Mentor Texts in Grades 6–8

The Informational Writing Toolkit
Using Mentor Texts in Grades 3–5

The Common Core Grammar Toolkit
Using Mentor Texts to Teach the Language Standards in Grades 6–8

The Common Core Grammar Toolkit
Using Mentor Texts to Teach the Language Standards in Grades 3–5

The Narrative Writing Toolkit

Using Mentor Texts in Grades 3–8

Sean Ruday

Routledge
Taylor & Francis Group
NEW YORK AND LONDON

First published 2016
by Routledge
711 Third Avenue, New York, NY 10017

and by Routledge
2 Park Square, Milton Park, Abingdon, Oxon, OX14 4RN

Routledge is an imprint of the Taylor & Francis Group, an informa business

© 2016 Taylor & Francis

The right of Sean Ruday to be identified as author of this work has been asserted by him in accordance with sections 77 and 78 of the Copyright, Designs and Patents Act 1988.

All rights reserved. The purchase of this copyright material confers the right on the purchasing institution to photocopy or download pages which bear the eResources icon and a copyright line at the bottom of the page. No other parts of this book may be reprinted or reproduced or utilized in any form or by any electronic, mechanical, or other means, now known or hereafter invented, including photocopying and recording, or in any information storage or retrieval system, without permission in writing from the publishers.

Trademark notice: Product or corporate names may be trademarks or registered trademarks, and are used only for identification and explanation without intent to infringe.

Library of Congress Cataloging in Publication Data
Names: Ruday, Sean, author.
Title: The narrative writing toolkit : using mentor texts in grades 3-8 /
    by Sean Ruday.
Description: New York : Routledge, 2016. | Includes bibliographical
    references.
Identifiers: LCCN 2015040515 | ISBN 9781138101524 (hardback) |
    ISBN 9781138101531 (pbk) | ISBN 9781315656885 (ebk)
Subjects: LCSH: Narration (Rhetoric)—Study and teaching (Elementary)
    | English language—Composition and exercises—Study and
    teaching (Elementary)
Classification: LCC LB1576 .R778 2016 | DDC 372.6/044—dc23
LC record available at http://lccn.loc.gov/2015040515

ISBN: 978-1-138-10152-4 (hbk)
ISBN: 978-1-138-10153-1 (pbk)
ISBN: 978-1-315-65688-5 (ebk)

Typeset in Palatino and Formata
by Swales & Willis Ltd, Exeter, Devon, UK

Contents

Meet the Author vii
Acknowledgments vii
eResources ix

Introduction: The New Era of Narrative Writing 1

Section 1: Narrative Writing Strategies Aligned with the Common Core State Standards for Grades 3–8 .... **11**

   1   Engaging and Orienting the Reader 13

   2   Organizing an Event Sequence 25

   3   Developing Experiences and Events. 37

   4   Incorporating Characterization 49

   5   Including Transitional Language 59

   6   Using Concrete Words and Phrases 71

   7   Creating Sensory Details 83

   8   Crafting a Strong Conclusion. 95

Section 2: Putting It Together. **107**

   9   Assessment Strategies. 109

  10   Final Thoughts and Recommendations for Classroom Practice. 117

Section 3: Resources. **123**

Appendix A: Reproducible Charts and Forms You Can Use in
   Your Classroom 125
Appendix B: A Guide for Book Studies 141
Annotated Bibliography: Excerpts from Published Works Featured in
   This Book, Aligned with Specific Common Core Standards. 143
References 159

Meet the Author

Sean Ruday is Assistant Professor of English Education at Longwood University. He began his teaching career at a public school in Brooklyn, NY, and has taught English and language arts in New York, Massachusetts, and Virginia. Sean is Co-President of the Assembly for the Teaching of English Grammar—a grammar-focused affiliate of the National Council of Teachers of English. He is the founder and editor of the *Journal of Literacy Innovation*. Some publications in which his articles have appeared are: *Journal of Teaching Writing, Journal of Language and Literacy Education, Contemporary Issues in Technology and Teacher Education,* and the *Yearbook of the Literacy Research Association.* His professional website is seanruday.weebly. com. You can follow him on Twitter @SeanRuday. This is his fifth book with Routledge Eye on Education.

Acknowledgments

I am thankful for all of the support I received while writing this book. I greatly appreciate the administrators and teachers who shared their thoughts, and gave me the opportunity to work with them and their students. Similarly, I am grateful to the wonderful students in the classes described in this book, who eagerly dove into the ideas and tools of narrative writing. I would also like to thank the students whose writings are included in this book; I am thrilled to feature their works. I am very thankful for this book's editor, Lauren Davis, whose guidance and encouragement has been invaluable to my writing career. I would like to thank my parents, Bob and Joyce Ruday, for all that they have done for me. I also want to thank my wife, Clare Ruday, who brightens my life by bringing humor and happiness to it.

eResources

The appendices of this book can be downloaded and printed for classroom use. You can access these downloads by visiting the book product page on our website: www.routledge.com/9781138101531. Then click on the tab that says "eResources" and select the files. They will begin downloading to your computer.

Introduction

The New Era of Narrative Writing

It's late in the evening on an early April Wednesday. I'm walking through the parking lot adjacent to the elementary and middle schools where I'm working with teachers and administrators on narrative writing. I'm grimacing in the spring wind, but my facial expression changes to a smile as I look at my phone and see a text message from the elementary school's principal: "Awesome work today. You did a great job easing everyone's minds about narrative writing. Both our teachers and our parents are feeling much better now."

This text message refers to the two workshops I conducted that day: one for teachers and another for parents. Before school began that morning, I led a professional development meeting for the elementary and middle-school literacy teachers on narrative writing and the Common Core State Standards (CCSS). In this meeting, a number of teachers expressed concern that they were unsure how to teach narrative writing in the CCSS era. A fifth-grade teacher named Alexis shared her concern:

> Please help me! I know I'm supposed to be teaching argument and informational writing, but narrative writing is a part of the Common Core too. We've gotten a bunch of resources on teaching the other genres, but I'd really love some guidance on how to teach narrative writing in today's day and age. Like, what parts of narrative writing should I focus on? What are the best ways to do focus on those parts?

Alexis' concerns were echoed by other teachers in the room, including a third-grade teacher named Julie who explained,

> There's a lot of change in writing instruction with the new [Common Core State] standards, and this change has brought a lot of anxiety. We used to teach narrative writing in really whatever way we wanted, but now things are different. There are all of these new, specific writing standards and I for one am anxious about how to teach narrative writing in ways that match what the Common Core wants.

At first, these comments struck me as a bit surprising; I thought to myself, *Isn't narrative writing the genre with which teachers are most comfortable? Why this anxiety?* However, after reflecting on Alexis and Julie's statements, I understood their concerns. "I get what you're saying," I replied. "We

♦ 1

writing teachers love teaching narrative writing and know how important it is for our students as they grow and develop as writers, but a lot of us are unsure—especially in today's changed educational landscape—of how to make sure that our narrative-writing instruction aligns with the Common Core State Standards. That's why I'm here: I'm going to be working with all of you—in workshop sessions like this one and in your classes with your students—to help you deliver outstanding narrative-writing instruction that correlates with the Common Core State Standards."

"Fantastic!" exclaimed Alexis. I could feel the mood in the room change from anxious and wary to comfortable and excited. I then proceeded to spend a wonderful day with several of the school's teachers and their students. We discussed the attributes of effective narrative writing, talked about the expectations of the CCSS, and began to explore the narrative-writing work we would do together.

After the school day ended, I began my second workshop of the day: a conversation with elementary and middle-school parents about narrative writing and the Common Core State Standards. In this meeting, a number of parents explained that they had heard the CCSS were a way to get rid of narrative writing in schools. "There's a lot of confusion about the Common Core State Standards," I said to the parents. "Some people think that these standards say that narrative writing doesn't matter, but that isn't the case at all. The CCSS say that students should write argumentative, informational, *and* narrative pieces. In fact, the standards suggest that students in fourth grade spend 35% of their writing time working on narratives, 35% of their writing time on informational writing, and 30% of their writing time on argument writing (Common Core State Standards, 2010). So, narrative writing is still alive and well in the age of the Common Core Standards!"

A number of parents nodded and some commented that they were relieved to learn this information. "You hear so much about the Common Core, but you don't always know what the truth is," replied one father. "My daughter loves telling stories. I'm really glad to know students still get to write narratives."

"They definitely do," I responded. "I'm thrilled to be working with your children and their teachers on narrative writing. We'll be looking at examples of strong narratives, talking about what makes them effective, and trying out the strategies that published authors use. We'll write narratives that align with the objectives of the Common Core State Standards while also valuing students' creativity and love for storytelling."

I've included this account of my experience meeting teachers and parents to frame the purpose and focus of this book. I decided to write this book to provide a resource for elementary and middle-school teachers who are looking to teach narrative writing in the age of the Common Core State Standards. As mentioned in the preceding vignette, narrative writing is still a significant part of the elementary and middle-school writing curriculum; teachers just need to understand what narrative-writing strategies the CCSS expect students to learn, and the best instructional methods to help students learn these strategies. The Common Core State Standards' expectations for narrative writing are specific and cover topics such as engaging and orienting the reader, organizing an event sequence, using concrete words and phrases, and crafting a strong conclusion. In many ways, these narrative-writing standards aren't much different from what many teachers have been doing, but they do represent specific, comprehensive expectations about what should be covered in particular grade levels. That's where this book comes in—to provide guidance for teachers as they facilitate their students' mastery of these concepts! It presents research-based and classroom-tested ideas designed to help elementary and middle-school teachers use examples of published narrative works to deepen their students' understandings of the key components of this genre, and ultimately, to help their students apply the strategies used by published authors to their own narrative writings.

This introductory chapter is divided into the following sections, each of which addresses a key aspect of this book's approach:

- ◆ The value of narrative writing
- ◆ The importance of mentor texts to narrative-writing instruction
- ◆ The toolkit metaphor
- ◆ The gradual release of responsibility
- ◆ What to expect in this book, including the specific Common Core State Standards this book addresses.

The Value of Narrative Writing

My conversations with teachers, parents, and administrators (such as those described at the opening of this Introduction) often reveal a belief that narrative writing has taken on a diminished role in today's schools. English education professor and researcher Rob Montgomery (2013) writes that narrative writing has taken on "orphan child" status in some places, as educational resources and workshops focus primarily on argument and informational writing. Like many other literacy experts, Montgomery advocates the value of narrative writing, arguing that narrative writing calls for students to think in ways that are just as rigorous and complex as other genres. While it may surprise some, the Common Core State Standards also assert that narrative writing is valuable and important; Appendix A of the English CCSS identifies a number of valuable attributes of narrative writing, such as: it can be used for a variety of purposes (such as to entertain, inform, or persuade); it can be applied to a range of subjects such as science and history/social studies; and it often utilizes complex writing strategies, such as the uses of dialogue and interior monologue to help readers make inferences about characters' personalities (Common Core State Standards, 2010).

Another significant aspect of narrative writing is the way it lends itself to use of 21st-century literacies: Bogard and McMackin (2012) explain that students as young as elementary school can use digital tools to plan and share narratives. Similarly, Dalton (2012) states that narrative writing in the 21st century can be enhanced by multimedia that allow authors to provide additional information that they may not be able to convey solely through the written word. The multimedia enhancements Dalton describes facilitate creativity and can engage students who, previously, may not have been interested in writing. In this book, we'll see these important features of narrative writing in action: we will meet students who craft narratives in their social studies and science courses, and also examine specific ways students incorporate multimedia (such as video clips and images that capture key narrative components) to enhance their works. In many of the book's chapters, you'll notice textboxes called "New Literacy Connection"; these figures identify specific ways students can make connections to technology and multimedia while crafting their narratives. Now that we've explored these valuable attributes of narrative writing, let's examine the best ways to teach this genre!

The Importance of Mentor Texts to Narrative Writing Instruction

An especially effective, research-based way to help our students master the narrative-writing strategies identified by the Common Core State Standards is to show them examples of high-quality narratives from which they can learn, and help them analyze the strategies used in these examples. These examples, called "mentor texts," provide students with clear models of what strong narrative writing looks like, and can spark discussions about how published narrative writers create effective pieces. Once students understand the strategies used by published writers, they can apply those same ideas to their own works.

Mentor texts are based on the idea that writers learn by reading outstanding texts in a particular genre or style, and then imitate the strategies used by other authors in their own works (Killgallon & Killgallon, 2013). This approach can be used with all modes of writing instruction, but this book focuses specifically on taking a mentor-text-focused approach to narrative writing, identifying key strategies for composing strong narratives, and considering how mentor texts can best be used to teach students those strategies. For example, I recently observed a teacher named Marie, who was working with her sixth graders on using sensory details (one of the Common Core State Standards for narrative writing). To help her students grasp this concept, Marie showed them the following passage from Maniac Magee by Jerry Spinelli (1990): "They were members of the town's trash-collecting corps, and as they huffed and bent to lay the box over the hole, they smelled vaguely of pine and rotten fruit" (p. 116).

After displaying and reading aloud this example, Marie worked with her students to identify language in the passage that appeals to the senses, helping them notice how Spinelli enables readers to imagine how the situation described in this passage sounds ("they huffed"), looks ("bent to lay the box over the hole"), and smells ("they smelled vaguely of pine and rotten fruit"). Mentor texts such as this one give students concrete understandings of what specific writing strategies look like in practice, and provide them with clear models of these strategies they can emulate in their own works. While Marie could have explained sensory imagery to her students without the benefit of this passage from Maniac Magee, her instruction wouldn't have been as clear and accessible as it was with the mentor text. In Marie's words, "I could tell something clicked for [the students] when I showed them that example. It's like that for me a lot when I teach with mentor texts. Showing students mentor text examples just helps them get writing strategies so much better."

The Toolkit Metaphor

A key component of the instructional approach described in the book is the toolkit metaphor: a conceptual framework for understanding the importance and uses of specific narrative-writing strategies. I believe that the writing strategies effective narrative writers use are comparable to the tools that craftspeople use to achieve specific tasks; just as a craftsperson would use a screwdriver in one situation and a saw in another, a successful narrative writer would use the strategy of including transitional language at an appropriate point in a piece of writing, and the strategy of crafting a strong conclusion at another point. In each instance, the author uses narrative writing strategies in specific situations to make their work as effective as possible.

I've found the toolkit approach to be very effective with the elementary and middle-school students with whom I work; it gives them a way to understand how writers use particular strategies, and the reasons why specific strategies are used in certain situations. When recently introducing this metaphor to a group of fifth graders, I explained:

Imagine that you're trying to put together a toy airplane; you wouldn't just take a hammer and start hammering everything. You'd look at how to assemble the toy and figure out which tool you need at each step. Writing's just like that. You'll learn different writing strategies, like how to 'hook' the reader, but you also will learn that some strategies are appropriate at some points in the pieces you write and other strategies are better suited for other points. Part of being a good writer is know when to use a certain writing strategy—or writing tool—just like part of building something is knowing which tool to use at each step in the process.

After I shared this information with the students, I was thrilled by their enthusiastic and thoughtful responses: "That's really cool," replied one student, a young man sitting in the back of the classroom. "I never would have thought about writing and building a toy as similar, but I get what you're saying."

"Yeah," responded a female student. "This makes me think about writing in a new way: all the [writing strategies] we learn are like tools for building good writing."

These students' comments reveal their understanding of the toolkit approach to writing instruction; each student's response shows a metacognitive awareness of how authors use writing strategies with specific purposes in mind. When used effectively, the end result of these strategies' uses is a well-crafted piece, just as the final product created by a skillful craftsperson is a well-constructed object. In this book, we'll examine how the narrative-writing strategies identified by the Common Core State Standards can function as tools that our students can use to craft effective fiction and nonfiction narratives that are not only well-written, but also reveal excellent understandings of the uses and purposes of important writing strategies.

The Gradual Release of Responsibility

The gradual release of responsibility method of instruction (Pearson & Gallagher, 1983) is an excellent tactic for helping students understand and use specific narrative-writing tools in their works. This instructional method, which requires students to take increased ownership of their learning, consists of three major stages. In the first stage, the teacher takes on most of the responsibility by presenting a writing strategy to students, explaining it to them, and showing them specific examples of it. In the second stage, teachers and students share responsibility through interactive learning activities. At this point in the instructional process, students might work as a whole class or in small groups, to identify examples of particular writing strategies and discuss the significance of those strategies. Finally, once the teacher feels the students are ready to do so, students take on the majority of the learning responsibility by working on a particular writing strategy independently. For example, teachers might ask students to use a strategy in narratives they are writing and reflect on how that strategy impacts the quality of the piece. Teachers still evaluate students' understanding in this final stage, but do so in more individualized ways, such as through one-on-one writing conferences that offer personalized feedback.

I recently met with a middle-school teacher named Hannah, who shared the success she and her students have experienced with the gradual release of responsibility method of writing instruction. According to Hannah, this instructional method was what her writing instruction needed to maximize its effectiveness:

Introduction ♦ 7

This way of teaching is exactly what I need! I've been showing students examples of writing strategies, but my writing instruction would just stop there. I wasn't supporting them as they tried to apply those strategies to their own writing. I taught my students about strong verbs a couple days ago, and I used the gradual release of responsibility. It was great—my students weren't overwhelmed and did a great job of using strong verbs when they wrote.

The instructional recommendations described in this book follow the gradual release of responsibility method that Hannah used in her class, providing specific suggestions for explaining the tools of narrative writing to your students, working with them as they become more familiar with these tools, and ultimately "turning the students loose" to apply these strategies to their own narratives (and supporting them while they do so).

What to Expect in This Book

This book identifies key tools that the Common Core State Standards say students need to be able to use in order to become effective narrative writers, and discusses specific, classroom-ready practices to help students in grades three through eight acquire these tools. It is divided into three sections:

♦ Section 1 focuses on narrative-writing strategies aligned with the Common Core Standards for grades three through eight. Each of the eight chapters in this section addresses an important element of narrative writing, and explains how to help your students grasp that concept. For consistency and ease of use, I've organized each chapter in this section in the following format:
  ♦ An introduction to the chapter's focal concept. This opening section provides a description and some examples of the writing strategy addressed in the chapter.
  ♦ A discussion of why the concept is important to strong narrative writing. This section explains why authors use this particular concept when writing narratives, and includes mentor examples from published works to illustrate how it looks in practice.
  ♦ A classroom snapshot. Each snapshot contains a description of my experiences teaching the chapter's focal concept to an elementary or middle-school class. I've included these snapshots so you can see how I taught my students about these important aspects of narrative writing, and can learn from these concrete examples as you work with your own students.
  ♦ Specific instructional recommendations. Each chapter closes with specific recommendations for you to keep in mind when engaging your students in learning activities that focus on these concepts.

8 ◆ Introduction

- ◆ Section 2 focuses on "Putting It Together." One chapter in this section focuses on strategies and easy-to-follow rubrics to use when assessing your students' narrative writing, while another chapter addresses final thoughts and tips that will help you as you put the ideas and recommendations, described in this book, into practice in your own classroom.
- ◆ Section 3 features the following resources designed to help you put this book's ideas into action:
  - ◆ Appendix A, which contains reproducible charts and forms you can use in your classroom.
  - ◆ Appendix B, which contains a guide for teachers and administrators interested in using this book for a book study.
  - ◆ An annotated bibliography, which includes excerpts from the published mentor texts featured in this book, the aspect of effective argument writing featured in each example, and the Common Core State Standard associated with that concept.
  - ◆ The book's reference list.

The table below lists the aspects of narrative writing described in this book, the chapters in which they are discussed, and the Common Core State Writing Standards for grades three through eight with which each aligns.

Table 1 Chapter Overview Table

Aspect of Narrative Writing	Chapter	Related Common Core State Writing Standards
Engaging and orienting the reader	Chapter 1	W.3.3.A, W.4.3.A, W.5.3.A, W.6.3.A, W.7.3.A, W.8.3.A
Organizing an event sequence	Chapter 2	W.3.3.A, W.4.3.A, W.5.3.A, W.6.3.A, W.7.3.A, W.8.3.A
Developing experiences and events	Chapter 3	W.3.3.B, W.4.3.B, W.5.3.B, W.6.3.B, W.7.3.B, W.8.3.B
Incorporating characterization	Chapter 4	W.3.3.B, W.4.3.B, W.5.3.B, W.6.3.B, W.7.3.B, W.8.3.B
Including transitional language	Chapter 5	W.3.3.C, W.4.3.C, W.5.3.C, W.6.3.C, W.7.3.C, W.8.3.C
Using concrete words and phrases	Chapter 6	W.4.3.D, W.5.3.D, W.6.3.D, W.7.3.D, W.8.3.D
Creating sensory details	Chapter 7	W.4.3.D, W.5.3.D, W.6.3.D, W.7.3.D, W.8.3.D
Crafting a strong conclusion	Chapter 8	W.3.3.E, W.4.3.E, W.5.3.E, W.6.3.E, W.7.3.E, W.8.3.E

Narrative writing remains an important component of the writing curriculum in the Common Core era, but now teachers need to understand what narrative-writing strategies the CCSS value, and the most effective ways to teach those strategies. Teaching narrative writing in ways that align with the Common Core State Standards and utilize research-based best practices is no easy task, but this book will give you the resources and advice you need to do so. In this book, we'll look together at the key aspects of strong narrative writing, what those aspects are, why they are important, how they are used in published examples of narrative writing, and specific ways to put them into practice in your classroom. My goal is for you to finish this book and understand the following ideas:

1. Narrative writing is integral to our students' successes and futures as writers.
2. Narrative writing continues to have a great deal of value in today's educational landscape.
3. Narrative writing is best taught with a toolkit approach that utilizes mentor texts and the gradual release of responsibility.

If you're ready to learn the best ways to teach your students narrative writing strategies that align with the Common Core State Standards, then keep reading!

Section 1

Narrative Writing Strategies Aligned with the Common Core State Standards for Grades 3–8

1

Engaging and Orienting the Reader

What Does "Engaging and Orienting the Reader" Mean?

A strong piece of narrative writing begins by engaging the reader in the story and orienting them with key information about the characters, setting, and situation. The Common Core State Writing Standards highlight the importance of this concept, as Standards W.3.3.A, W.4.3.A, W.5.3.A, W.6.3.A, W.7.3.A, and W.8.3.A emphasize the significance of effectively engaging and orienting readers of narratives. In this chapter, we'll discuss the following: what "engaging and orienting the reader" means; why this concept is important for effective narrative writing; a description of a lesson on this concept; and key recommendations for helping your students engage and orient readers of their own narrative writings. Along the way, we'll examine how published authors engage and orient readers to their narratives, and explore what makes those authors' works especially effective.

We'll begin by considering what it means to engage and orient readers to a piece of narrative writing. The first of these components—engaging the reader—captures the reader's interest and encourages them to want to continue with the piece. The second—orienting the reader—begins to introduce important information about the narrative, such as who the main characters are, where the story takes place, and what is taking place. Language that engages and orients readers provides two significant elements of narrative writing: the hook and the first look. Table 1.1 describes each of these elements.

♦ 13

14 ◆ Narrative Writing Strategies

Table 1.1 Key Elements of Engaging and Orienting Readers

Element	Description
The hook	The hook to a piece of narrative writing is language that is intended to capture the reader's attention. A book's hook is generally found in its opening lines and is used to "pull in" the reader so that they will continue reading the narrative.
The first look	A piece's first look is typically found immediately following the hook and introduces key aspects of the piece's narrative, such as its characters, setting, and situation. It doesn't provide detailed discussion of these aspects of the piece, but does begin to give the reader an initial understanding of what is taking place.

Now, let's examine how author Kate DiCamillo engages and orients her readers by providing a hook and first look at the beginning of her novel *The Tale of Despereaux*:

> This story begins within the walls of a castle, with the birth of a mouse. A small mouse. The last mouse born to his parents and the only one of his litter to be born alive.
> "Where are my babies?" said the exhausted mother when the ordeal was through. "Show to me my babies."
> The father mouse held the one small mouse up high.
> "There is only this one," he said. "The others are dead."
>
> (DiCamillo, 2003: p. 11)

In this passage, DiCamillo engages, or hooks, her readers with three opening sentences: "This story begins within the walls of a castle, with the birth of a mouse. A small mouse. The last mouse born to his parents and the only one of his litter to be born alive." These sentences grab the reader's attention with a few introductory statements about a mouse. Readers who encounter these opening points may keep reading to learn about the importance of this mouse, and why he is the only one of his litter to live. After these opening lines, DiCamillo orients the reader to some of the characters in the text by providing a first look at a conversation between a mother and father mouse. By incorporating this conversation, DiCamillo helps readers begin to develop an initial understanding of what is taking place. In this chapter's next section, we'll examine how the strategies of engaging and orienting the reader are especially important to effective narrative writing.

Why Engaging and Orienting the Reader Is Important to Effective Narrative Writing

The writing tools of engaging and orienting the reader are integral to the success of a piece of narrative writing. If authors did not employ these

Engaging and Orienting the Reader ◆ 15

Table 1.2 Importance of Language that Engages and Orients Readers in *The Tale of Despereaux*

Excerpt from Text	Why it Is Important to the Narrative
This story begins within the walls of a castle, with the birth of a mouse. A small mouse. The last mouse born to his parents and the only one of his litter to be born alive.	This excerpt is important because of the way it draws in the reader. Kate DiCamillo uses this language to engage the reader in the piece and pique their interest so that they will keep reading. Without this excerpt, DiCamillo's book wouldn't engage readers as effectively at the beginning of the narrative.
"Where are my babies?" said the exhausted mother when the ordeal was through. "Show to me my babies." The father mouse held the one small mouse up high. "There is only this one," he said. "The others are dead."	This except is important because of the way it transitions readers from the opening hook to the events of the narrative. Through the description of this conversation, DiCamillo introduces the opening events of Despereaux's life and sets up the rest of the narration that will follow. Without this text, the book would lack a logical transition from its opening lines to the rest of the piece's narrative and the characters related to it.

strategies, it would be much more difficult for readers to engage with and understand their works. For example, if Kate DiCamillo did not engage and orient us readers at the beginning of *The Tale of Despereaux*, we would struggle with the opening of the book because there wouldn't be anything in the text that draws us in, or introduces us to key aspects of the situation. While it's possible that some readers would eventually figure out what is taking place, it's also very likely that many readers would grow confused and frustrated by the fact that the author did not engage and orient readers, and would therefore stop reading. Table 1.2 explains why the language in *The Tale of Despereaux* that engages and orients readers is especially important to the piece.

As this table describes, these opening passages are essential to the reader's engagement in and understanding of *The Tale of Despereaux*: they reveal Kate DiCamillo's ability to grab the attention of her readers and orient them to key elements of a narrative. To further illustrate the importance of the narrative-writing tools of engaging and orienting readers, let's explore how Lemony Snicket uses these strategies in the opening of *The Bad Beginning* (the first book in his *A Series of Unfortunate Events* sequence). First, let's take a look at the opening text of this book:

If you are interested in stories with happy endings, you would be better off reading some other book. In this book, not only is there no happy ending, there is no happy beginning and very few happy things happen in the middle. This is because not very many happy things happened in the lives of the three Baudelaire youngsters.

Violet, Klaus, and Sunny Baudelaire were intelligent children, and they were charming, and resourceful, and had pleasant facial features, but they were extremely unlucky, and most everything that happened to them was rife with misfortunate, misery, and despair.

(Snicket, 1999: p.1)

Lemony Snicket uses the first two sentences of this opening passage to hook the reader, as statements such as "If you are interested in stories with happy endings, you would be better off reading some other book" can intrigue potential readers, and encourage them to continue with the book. After these surprising and engaging first lines, Snicket begins to introduce the book's characters and the challenges they face. Language such as "they were extremely unlucky, and most everything that happened to them was rife with misfortunate, misery, and despair" gives readers an opening look at the book's events.

This excerpt from *The Bad Beginning* is a great example of the importance of engaging and orienting readers to effective narrative writing; without the text that hooks readers, and without the information that gives them a first look at the Baudelaire orphans' situation, readers' experiences with *The Bad Beginning* would vary significantly from their current ones. As this book is currently constructed, Lemony Snicket prepares his readers for the story he will tell in *The Bad Beginning*, by capturing their attention and providing information about the forthcoming challenges they will face (using an amusing and irreverent tone to do so). Without the language that performs these functions, readers would not be introduced to the book's characters and events in the effective way that they currently are. In the next section, we'll take a look inside a third-grade classroom and examine how the students in that class consider the importance of this writing strategy.

A Classroom Snapshot

"Since we've been talking about how authors engage and orient readers," I tell my third graders, "I've been thinking about this in everything I read. Yesterday, I was reading *Charlotte's Web* to one of my children and I was so struck by the way the author engages and orients readers that I wanted to bring it in to share it with all of you."

The students smile, interested to see how the author of *Charlotte's Web*, E.B. White, utilizes this strategy. These students and I have spent the past few classes discussing the narrative-writing strategy of engaging and orienting readers. On our first day working on this concept, I introduced this strategy to the students, explaining that when narrative writers engage and orient their readers, they provide a hook designed to interest readers in the story, and then a first look meant to introduce readers to some aspect of the piece. Next, we spent two class periods discussing why this strategy is important to effective narrative writing; we looked at the examples from *The Tale of Despereaux* and *The Bad Beginning*, discussed in this chapter, examined how those passages engage and orient writers, and talked about why doing so is important to those narratives. Today, I'm going to give the students more responsibility for their learning through the use of an interactive lesson: after the students and I discuss the language in *Charlotte's Web* that engages and orients readers, I'll divide them into groups, and ask each group to work together to do the same kind of identification and analysis with published texts they choose.

"Let's take a look at the opening of *Charlotte's Web*," I tell the students, placing the book on the document camera and projecting the following text to the rest of the room:

> "Where's Papa going with that ax?" said Fern to her mother as they were setting the table for breakfast.
>
> "Out to the hoghouse," replied Mrs. Arable. "Some pigs were born last night."
>
> "I don't see why he needs an ax," continued Fern, who was only eight.
>
> "Well," said her mother, "one of the pigs is a runt. It's very small and weak, and it will never amount to anything. So your father has decided to do away with it."
>
> (White, 1952, p. 1)

I read the text out loud as the students follow along and then ask, "What parts of this passage do you think the author is using to try to engage readers?"

Thrilled to see a number of student hands fly up around the room, I call on a young lady who answers, "The question in the first sentence. I think that's supposed to engage us."

"Well said," I reply. "Why do you all think that the question in the first sentence is meant to engage readers?"

"Because," responds another student, "it makes you wonder what the answer to the question is."

"Nicely put," I tell the student. "Putting a question at the beginning of a narrative, like E.B. White does here in *Charlotte's Web*, is a great way to get a reader's attention because, as you said, readers will wonder what the answer is to that question, which gets them engaged in the piece.

"So," I continue, addressing the whole class, "if that part is meant to engage us, what language in this passage does E.B. White use to orient us to the situation in this narrative?"

"I think the rest of [the passage] does that, especially the parts about the pig," states a student sitting in the front of the class.

"Why do you think that is?" I inquire. "Why do you think the rest of this passage orients us to the situation?"

18 ♦ Narrative Writing Strategies

"Because," replies the student, "this book is about that pig. When the author mentions this pig, he's introducing us to the main character in the book."

"Yes," I say to the student. "E.B. White orients readers to the situation by introducing Wilbur, the pig that turns out to be the main character in *Charlotte's Web.* In addition, much of the action of this book focuses on keeping Wilbur alive; we can see that issue brought up here on the book's first page. You all did a great job thinking about how different sections of the opening of *Charlotte's Web* engage and orient readers. Now, I'm going to ask you to do the same thing in small groups with the openings of other books. We're going to divide into groups of four and each group is going to analyze how the author of the book you choose engages and orients readers. To get started, you'll select a text from our classroom library. Then, you'll look at its opening with your small group members, and talk with your group members about what part of the opening is meant to engage readers and what part is meant to orient readers. After that, you'll want to talk about how you can tell which part of the book's opening engages, and what part orients. I'm going to give each group a graphic organizer that will help guide your thinking. You'll fill this graphic organizer out as you work and I'll come around and check in with each group."

I place the graphic organizer (Table A1, Appendix A) on the document camera so that students can see exactly what they'll be doing as the work on this activity (see Appendix A for a reproducible version of this graphic organizer).

Once I've gone over the components of this graphic organizer with the students and divided them into groups, I ask the student groups to begin by selecting books from the classroom library. The students then start to analyze the books' openings for our focal strategies of engaging and orienting readers. After each group has taken some time to discuss these ideas, I begin to sit down with them and ask what they've noticed. I first meet with a group that is using Ruth Stiles Gannett's (1950) novel *Elmer and the Dragon.*

"How's it going so far?" I begin.

"Awesome," responds a boy in the group. "This book's beginning is really cool. Check it out." This student proceeds to share the opening paragraph of *Elmer and the Dragon,* which reads:

Into the evening sky flew Elmer Elevator aboard the gentle baby dragon, leaving Wild Island behind forever. Elmer, who was nine years old, had just rescued the dragon from the ferocious animals who lived on the island. An old alley cat told him how the dragon had been hurt when he fell from a cloud onto the island, and how the wild animals had made him their miserable prisoner. Elmer, feeling sorry for the dragon, and also hoping to fly on his back, had set off to the rescue.

(Gannett, 1950, p. 1)

"That is a really cool beginning," I concur. "Now, let's talk about what you noticed. What text did you notice here that you think is meant to engage readers?"

"The first line," replies a group member. "That definitely engages readers. It puts you right in the action of Elmer flying on a dragon. I can tell it's supposed to engage people who are reading because of the action in it—starting in the middle of action is really engaging."

"Very nice," I praise the student's explanation. "I love that you not only identified the text that the author uses to engage readers, but also explained how you can tell that text is meant to engage readers. Make sure you write those great ideas down on your graphic organizer."

The student nods and I move our discussion to the next part of the analysis: "In addition to thinking about how authors engage readers, we're also thinking about how they orient their readers. What text in this paragraph do you think the author uses to orient readers?"

"Oh, I know!" exclaims a student in the group. "It's the rest of the paragraph. The rest of this paragraph orients because it says who Elmer is and why he's with the dragon."

"Excellent," I respond. "That's very well said. Like you explained, we can tell the rest of this paragraph—that is, the text after the first sentence—is meant to orient readers because of the way it gives background information on both Elmer and the dragon. Make sure you write down your ideas on this topic on your handout as well. You all did a great job thinking about this!"

I continue to circulate around the classroom, checking in with the other groups of students. Finding myself similarly impressed with the quality of the other groups' works, I praise their efforts: "Everyone in here did a fantastic job today! Each group did such a nice job of picking out text meant to engage and orient readers, and then explaining how you can tell that the text you picked out does so. It's hard to both identify language that does this and explain why, but you all did it so well. Tomorrow, we're going to start working on writing our own narrative openings that engage and orient readers—I can't wait to see your work!"

Recommendations for Teaching Students About Engaging and Orienting Readers

In this section, I describe a step-by-step instructional process to use when teaching students about engaging and orienting readers in narrative writing. The instructional steps I recommend are:

1. Show students examples of published narratives that engage and orient readers.
2. Talk with students about why engaging and orienting readers is important to effective narrative writing.

20 ♦ Narrative Writing Strategies

3. Have students analyze how published authors engage and orient readers.
4. Work with students as they engage and orient readers in their own narrative writing.
5. Help students reflect on why engaging and orienting readers is important to their own narratives.

Each of these recommendations is described in detail in this section.

1. Show students examples of published narratives that engage and orient readers.

This initial step of this instructional process is an excellent way to introduce students to a writing strategy in a clear and engaging way. Fletcher and Portalupi (2001) advocate that students examine published examples of specific writing tactics: they compare writing instruction with learning to ski or building a craft, and say students need to see expert models from which to learn. In my experience, most students do not grasp writing strategies through lectures and generalized explanations nearly as well as they do when they see examples of those strategies in action.

When I show published examples to my students, I talk with them about how the authors of those texts engage readers and orient them to the situation in the narrative. For example, when working recently with a class of third graders, I showed them the example from *The Tale of Despereaux*, described previously in this chapter, and led a discussion on how Kate DiCamillo engages us in the story, while also helping us develop an initial understanding of its characters. It's also important to note that using published examples can maximize student engagement; when I want to show my students how a published author engages and orients their readers in a narrative, I'll pick a grade-level text written by an author many of them enjoy. When students see a favorite author using a particular writing strategy, it can make them more motivated to try it in their own works as well.

2. Talk with students about why engaging and orienting readers is important to effective narrative writing.

Once you've shown your students examples of published narratives that engage and orient readers, and have discussed those examples with them, you'll be ready to move to the next step of this instructional process: talking with the students about why these writing strategies are important to effective narrative writing. To do this, I recommend working with students to identify specific excerpts from published texts that engage and orient readers, and then talking with them about why each excerpt is important to the author's narrative.

For example, my third graders and I discussed the importance of these writing strategies for the previously described opening paragraph of Lemony Snicket's *The Bad Beginning*; we identified the opening lines—"If you are interested in stories with happy endings, you would be better off reading some other book. In this book, not only is there no happy ending, there is no happy beginning and very few happy things happen in the middle"—as text intended to engage readers, and examined their significance to the entire narrative. Several students in the class commented on the importance of these lines; one explained, "These sentences are great at getting readers interested. They make you want to read and find out why the book doesn't have a happy ending." Another student remarked on Lemony Snicket's unique style: "This is a really different way to start a book. Most books don't start like this and I think that can make readers want to read more." These students' responses showed me that they understood why Lemony Snicket chose to begin his book in this way, and revealed their awareness of the significance of engaging readers when writing narratives.

3. Have students analyze how published authors engage and orient readers.

In the third step of this instructional process, I suggest placing increased responsibility on the students by asking them to work in small groups or individually to analyze how published writers engage and orient their readers. This activity—an example of which is described in this chapter's classroom snapshot—builds on the ideas discussed in the first two steps of the process, and calls for students to apply their knowledge of these writing strategies to their own analyses of published texts. I recommend asking students to select texts of their own choosing for analysis, as this can maximize student engagement in the task, and then giving each student or group the graphic organizer depicted in Table A1 (Appendix A), to guide them through their analysis. As the students work on analyzing the openings of published narratives, I circulate the room and check in with each of them.

When I meet with a student or a group, I make sure that they have not only identified excerpts from the book that are used to engage and orient readers, but also that they can explain how those excerpts perform those functions. Getting students to explain how an excerpt achieves a particular objective helps them think deeply about the ways authors achieve specific results in their work. The group I met with in the classroom snapshot did an excellent job of identifying how the examples they identified from *Elmer and the Dragon* engage and orient readers. Another group with which I spoke during that lesson did a similarly strong job analyzing the book *I was a Third-Grade Science Project* by Mary Jane Auch (1998); the students in that group explained that the book's opening line—"Having a genius for a friend can be real trouble" (p. 1)—is an excellent example of language that engages readers. "This is an awesome first sentence," shared a student in the group. "The author definitely uses it to get you interested and keep reading. You want to keep reading because you want to know why it can be [real trouble]."

4. Work with students as they engage and orient readers in their own narrative writing.

Now that your students have analyzed the ways published authors engage and orient readers to their narratives, it's time to ask the students to apply these tools to their own writing. When I reach this stage of the instructional process with my students, I tell them that their job is to write the opening paragraph of a narrative, being sure to include language that engages readers and information that orients them to key aspects of the rest of the narrative. I explain to the students that they can draw from the strategies that the published authors we've studied use to engage and orient their readers, but that they should also use their own creativity and ideas when composing their works.

A student with whom I recently worked applied these tools to his own writing in the following passage, which opens a fictional narrative he wrote about a young quarterback playing his first game for the Pittsburgh Steelers.

In a one-on-one writing conference, this student did a wonderful job of identifying language intended to engage readers and well as text meant to orient them: "I used the first sentence to engage readers. That's the one where Sam says his lifetime goal is really coming true. I thought this sentence would get readers interested because they'd want to know how his lifetime goal is coming true. I used the rest of the sentences in this paragraph to orient readers. In those sentences, I said a bunch of stuff about Sam being from Pittsburgh and loving the Steelers. Those sentences help readers know why this is important to Sam."

New Literacy Connection

This student author also commented on how he might use multimedia to enhance readers' experiences with the beginning of his narrative. He explained that he would like to include, at the opening of the narrative, a video clip of the Pittsburgh Steelers' fans cheering while the team is introduced: "I found a great video on YouTube of Steelers fans going crazy while the team comes out on the field. I want to put a link to it at the start of the story so people reading the story can know what Sam would have seen and heard when he ran onto the field."

Figure 1.1 Student Example of Text that Engages and Orients Readers

> "My lifetime goal is really coming true," thought Sam Rogers. As a kid growing up in Pittsburgh, Sam had dreamed of this day. He starred at quarterback in middle school, high school, and college. Now he was finally in the NFL playing quarterback for the Pittsburgh Steelers, his favorite team. Just like his heroes, former Steelers quarterbacks Terry Bradshaw and Ben Roethlisberger, Sam was ready to throw the ball for the black and yellow. He ran out onto the field with his teammates and couldn't wait for the game to begin.

5. Help students reflect on why engaging and orienting readers is important to their own narratives.

To guide students as they do this, I ask them to reflect on the following questions:

1. "Why is engaging and orienting the reader important to the narrative that you're writing?"
2. "How would your narrative be different without the sections that engage and orient the reader?"

Responding to these questions increases students' metacognitive awareness of this writing strategy, helping them see the significance of the narrative-writing tools of engaging and orienting readers. The student who wrote about the Pittsburgh Steelers player explained that these strategies are important to the narrative he's writing because, "engaging readers gets them interested in whatever story you're going to tell and orienting them helps them understand some things about the story. Like in my story, the first sentence is supposed to get readers interested and the rest of the first paragraph introduces Sam and talks about why playing quarterback for the Steelers is a big deal to him." He explained how his narrative would be different without the sections that engage and orient the reader by saying, "If I didn't write this paragraph, there's stuff you wouldn't know, like where Sam grew up and why playing for the

Steelers matters to him. I also wouldn't be able to engage readers, like I do in the first line." This student's responses reveal his awareness of the importance of engaging and orienting to readers to his specific piece, as well as to writing in general.

Final Thoughts on Engaging and Orienting Readers

- Engaging and orienting readers in narrative writing is addressed in Common Core State Writing Standards W.3.3.A, W.4.3.A, W.5.3.A, W.6.3.A, W.7.3.A, and W.8.3.A.
- The first of these components, engaging the reader, captures the reader's interest and encourages them to want to continue with the piece.
  - The section of a narrative that engages the reader can also be called the piece's "hook."
- The second component, orienting the reader, begins to introduce key information about the narrative, such as who the main characters are, where the story takes place, and what is taking place.
  - Text that orients the reader can also be called a piece's "first look."
- Engaging and orienting readers is especially important to a piece of narrative writing because of how these strategies help readers become interested in and understand the beginning of a story.
- Without these writing tools, readers would struggle because there wouldn't be anything in the text that draws them in, or introduces them to key aspects of a situation.
- When teaching students about engaging and orienting readers:
  - show students examples of published narratives that engage and orient readers;
  - talk with students about why engaging and orienting readers is important to effective narrative writing;
  - have students analyze how published authors engage and orient readers;
  - work with students as they engage and orient readers in their own narrative writing;
  - help students reflect on why engaging and orienting readers is important to their own narratives.

2

Organizing an Event Sequence

What Does "Organizing an Event Sequence" Mean?

In order for their works to be as effective as possible, narrative writers must think carefully about the order of events in their pieces. This writing strategy, also called "organizing an event sequence," is addressed in Common Core Writing Standards W.3.3.A, W.4.3.A, W.5.3.A, W.6.3.A, W.7.3.A, and W.8.3.A, and is an integral component of strong narrative writing. In this chapter, we'll explore the following: what "organizing an event sequence" means; why this concept is important to writing a strong narrative; a description of a lesson on this concept; and key recommendations for teaching your students to organize event sequences in their own narrative writing. Throughout the chapter, we'll look at how published authors organize event sequences in their own works and consider what makes those authors works particularly effective.

Let's begin by examining what it means to organize an event sequence in a piece of narrative writing. When a writer composes a narrative, they need to think about what will happen in their story *and* the order in which those events will take place. Some especially significant aspects of narrative sequence are identified and described in Table 2.1 below.

To compose a narrative effectively, an author will consider each of these components and structure the piece in a way that allows readers to clearly envision the order in which the story's key events take place. For example, in her book *Night of the Ninjas* (1995), Mary Pope Osborne begins the narrative by introducing Annie and Jack, the book's main characters, and incorporating ninjas into the story's plot. Osborne then transitions into the piece's rising action, in which Annie and Jack travel back in time to Japan and encounter ninjas, using the narration "Jack peeked

♦ 25

26 ♦ Narrative Writing Strategies

Table 2.1 Key Aspects of Narrative Sequence

Aspects of Narrative Sequence	Descriptions
Exposition	The exposition introduces key components of the story, such as important characters, setting aspects, and motivations.
Rising Action	In the rising action, the conflict in the story progresses.
Climax	In the climax, the story's conflict reaches its most intense point. It involves some pivotal event concerning the story's protagonist.
Falling Action	The events of the falling action are brought about by the action that took place in the story's climax. I call this stage the "dominoes that fall," due to the action in the climax.
Resolution	In the resolution, the conflict is resolved in some way and the events of the story reach a point of closure.

over the windowsill. His eyes met the dark eyes of the tall ninja" (p. 16) to describe these events. Next, Osborne moves readers to the book's climax, in which Jack and Annie are trapped by samurai warriors: "Jack and Annie crouched together. Samurai were on both sides of them now. They were trapped!" (p. 48). Throughout Osborne's narration, she orders the book's events clearly and effectively, in a way that allows readers to understand the sequence of her narrative.

Why Organizing an Event Sequence Is Important to Effective Narrative Writing

Organizing an event sequence is a key tool to a successful piece of narrative writing; if a narrative's events were disorganized, readers would not be able to determine when certain actions in the piece took place. Since the aspects of narrative sequence described in Table 2.1 are related to one another, a narrative without a clear sequence of events would produce confused, frustrated readers who might misunderstand the story entirely. For example, if Mary Pope Osborne began *Night of the Ninjas* with the piece's climax and then proceeded to the exposition, readers would not understand what was taking place. In addition, the narrative would not be as interesting since the aspects of the narrative sequence would not build on each other; for example, the exposition and rising action would no longer build up to the climax, and the resolution would seem out of place if it didn't occur at the end of the story.

Table 2.2 Key Aspects of Narrative Sequence and Corresponding Quotations from *Night of the Ninjas* (Presented in Original Order)

Aspects of Narrative Sequence	Corresponding Quotations from *Night of the Ninjas*
Exposition	*The magic tree house was back.* "Come on up!" Annie shouted. Jack ran to the rope ladder. He started climbing. (p. 5)
Rising Action	Jack peeked over the windowsill. His eyes met the dark eyes of the tall ninja. (p. 16)
Climax	Jack and Annie crouched together. Samurai were on both sides of them now. They were trapped! (p. 48)
Falling Action	"You have done well," the figure said. *It was the ninja master.* "You have followed the way of the ninja," he said. (p. 59)
Resolution	Together they took off through the cool, dark woods. They moved silently and swiftly—two shadow warriors returning home. (p. 69)

To illustrate the importance of organizing an event sequence, let's take a look at Tables 2.2 and 2.3. Table 2.2 lists the key aspects of narrative sequence in order, with quotations from *Night of the Ninjas* that correspond with each aspect, while Table 2.3 contains these same narrative aspects and quotations, but lists them *out* of order, showing how different the story would be if these components were not clearly organized.

The order of the quotations and narrative aspects in this table reveals the clear sequencing that Mary Pope Osborne uses in *Night of the Ninjas* to provide her readers with a well-organized and well-structured story. Conversely, the order of quotations and sequencing components in Table 2.3 provides a much different effect.

The contrast between these tables indicates the importance to narrative writing of organizing an event sequence clearly. Table 2.2, which aligns with the actual structure of *Night of the Ninjas,* is easy to understand, and engages readers by building up to a climax and then gradually moving to a resolution of the piece's conflict. However, if *Night of the Ninjas* was organized like Table 2.3, it would not only be difficult to understand, but would also reduce reader engagement, since the story would begin with the climax and move to the resolution shortly thereafter; with this structure, there would be little reason for the audience to keep reading!

In the next section, we'll take a look inside a fourth-grade classroom and examine how the students in this class apply their knowledge of organizing an event sequence.

28 ◆ Narrative Writing Strategies

Table 2.3 Key Aspects of Narrative Sequence and Corresponding Quotations from *Night of the Ninjas* (Presented Out of Order)

Aspects of Narrative Sequence	Corresponding Quotations from *Night of the Ninjas*
Climax	Jack and Annie crouched together. Samurai were on both sides of them now. They were trapped! (p. 48)
Exposition	*The magic tree house was back.* "Come on up!" Annie shouted. Jack ran to the rope ladder. He started climbing. (p. 5)
Resolution	Together they took off through the cool, dark woods. They moved silently and swiftly—two shadow warriors returning home. (p. 69)
Rising Action	Jack peeked over the windowsill. His eyes met the dark eyes of the tall ninja. (p. 16)
Falling Action	"You have done well," the figure said. *It was the ninja master.* "You have followed the way of the ninja," he said. (p. 59)

A Classroom Snapshot

"I want to start today's class," I tell my fourth graders, "by saying how proud I am of all of you. I say this because you've all done such great work so far in our conversations about organizing event sequences in narrative writing!"

Today is my third day working with this group of fourth graders on the narrative writing tool of effectively organizing event sequences. In our first class on the topic, I introduced this writing strategy to the students, talking with them about the key aspects of narrative sequence described in Table 2.1—exposition, rising action, climax, falling action, and resolution—and the features of each of these components. During our second meeting, the students and I discussed the importance, to effective narrative writing, of the strategy of organizing an event sequence. To illustrate the significance of this concept, I showed the students the quotations from *Night of the Ninjas* in Tables 2.2 and 2.3, and led them in a conversation about why it's important that Mary Pope Osborne organized her book in the way that she did.

In today's class, I'll give the students more responsibility for their work on this writing strategy by asking them to work in groups to identify the key aspects of narrative sequence in short stories, and then consider why the organization of these aspects is important to the effectiveness of the story. After I explain these directions to the students, I tell them, "This will give you a chance to put your understanding of organizing event sequences into action. You're going to use a familiar text for this activity—*Sideways Stories from Wayside School* (Sachar, 1978), which I know you read earlier this year." Several students cheer to indicate their fondness for the book. "I'll assign each group a story from this book to work on. To guide you as you do this activity," I continue, "I'm going to give you a handout to help you organize your thoughts and reflect on the importance of this concept." I place the graphic organizer (Table A2, Appendix A) on the document camera, projecting it to the front of the room. (See Appendix A for a reproducible version of this template that you can use with your classes).

"As you can see," I tell the students, "this graphic organizer asks you to identify quotes from your book that match up with each of the narrative sequence aspects on the left side of the chart. You'll write down text from the exposition, rising action, climax, falling action, and resolution. You can also see the reflection question at the bottom; once you complete the graphic organizer, I'd like you to think about that question and how it relates to your group's story.

"Before you work on this activity in your groups," I continue, "I'd like for all of us to work on an example together. We'll read a story as a class and identify sections of text from it that match up with each of the narrative sequence elements." I give each student a copy of the story "Mrs. Gorf" from *Sideways Stories from Wayside School*—a fun story about a teacher who turns her students into apples, later turns them back into humans, and is eventually turned into an apple herself—and read the piece aloud, asking students to follow along silently. When I finish reading, I say to the class: "Okay, now it's time to think about how Louis Sachar, the author of this story, organizes the sequence of events in this narrative. The first section on this graphic organizer up here on the document cam is 'Exposition.' Can anyone find some text from the exposition of this story?"

The class is quiet at first. After a few moments of silence, a student raises her hand and volunteers. "I think it's the part at the beginning of the story that says, 'Mrs. Gorf had a long tongue and pointed ears. She was the meanest teacher in Wayside School'" (p. 11).

"Correct," I reply, writing the excerpt she identified on the chart. "Why do you think this is the exposition?"

"Because it introduces Mrs. Gorf and tells us about her personality; that she's mean. Her meanness is a big part of the story."

"Well said," I respond. "Now, let's think about the rising action; the part that builds toward the climax. Does anyone have any thoughts on the rising action in this story?"

Several students raise their hands; I call on a young man who explains, "I think it's this part here where Mrs. Gorf starts turning the kids in the class into apples."

"Nice job," I tell the student. "Can you find any specific text that you'd identify as the rising action?"

30 ♦ Narrative Writing Strategies

"I think this part right here," the student replies, "that says, 'She wiggled her ears—first her right one, then her left—stuck out her tongue, and turned Joe into an apple'" (p. 12).

"Awesome," I say, praising the student's response. "Now, let's think about the climax of this story. Who can identify some text from this story's climax?"

This time, even more student hands fly into the air. A student shares, "I think it's when the students that Mrs. Gorf has turned into apples start attacking her. The story says, 'Mrs. Gorf fell on the floor. The apples jumped all over her'" (p. 14).

"Very good," I tell the student. "That's a really good job of identifying the climax. How did you know that's the climax of the story?"

"Because," the student replies, "it's the most intense part of the conflict between Mrs. Gorf and her students. The rising action of her turning them into apples built up to this climax."

"Wonderful explanation," I remark. "What do you all think about the story's falling action? Where is that?"

I call on a student at the back of the classroom who explains, "The falling action is after the climax when Mrs. Gorf turns the apples back into children. The sentence that explains it is right here: 'She stuck out her tongue, wiggled her ears—this time her left one first, then her right—and turned the apples back into children'" (p. 14).

"Fantastic," I say. "You did a great job of pointing out this falling action and identifying the text that goes along with it. Remember that the falling action leads us to the resolution, where the conflict is finally resolved and we have some kind of closure. Does anyone have any thoughts on what the story's resolution is?"

A student in the front of the room throws her hand in the air and tells the class, "The resolution is when Mrs. Gorf accidentally turns herself into an apple, and then another teacher comes in and eats the apple she turned herself into."

"Perfect," I praise the student's comment. "Can you find the text that goes along with the resolution you shared with us?"

"Sure," she responds. "First is the sentence that shows how Mrs. Gorf accidentally turned herself into an apple: 'But Jenny held up a mirror, and Mrs. Gorf turned herself into an apple' (p. 14). And then there's the part when another teacher comes in and eats it: 'He picked up the apple, which was really Mrs. Gorf, shined it up on his shirt, and ate it'" (p. 14).

"Great!" I exclaim. "All of you did excellent work on this. I love how well you identified events and excerpts from this story that go along with all of the narrative sequence aspects we've been talking about. You can see there's one thing left on our handout: the reflection question 'Why is it important that the text you used followed this narrative sequence?' What do you all think? Why is it important that this story followed this sequence?"

To my delight, almost all of the students in the class raise their hands. I first call on a student who explains, "It keeps you interested. We learn about Mrs. Gorf, start to not like her because she's mean, and then keep reading to find out what happened."

"Yeah," interjects another student. "The exposition and rising action get you interested. If the story didn't start with those, it wouldn't be as interesting and it wouldn't make sense really either."

"Those are fantastic responses. I'm so thrilled with your work today. Now, we're going to do the same thing in our groups. As I mentioned before, I'm going to give each group a handout and a story from *Sideways Stories from Wayside School.* Your job is to work with your group members to complete the handout, just like we just did together as a whole class. I'll come around and check in with each group as you work."

I circulate the room, continuing to be impressed with the students' work. When I meet with each group, I ask the students to summarize the story they're working with, and talk me through the information they recorded on their group's handout. "Tell me what quotation you noticed for each narrative sequence aspect," I say to each group. Once the students identify the quotation that corresponds to each element and explain why their group selected it, I ask the group to comment on the reflection question at the bottom of the handout that asks why it's important that the text the group used followed this narrative sequence. All of the student groups do a good job responding to this question, commenting on how the story they analyzed would not have made as much sense, or been as interesting, if author Louis Sachar did not organize the event sequence effectively in his works.

After meeting with each group, I tell the class how pleased I am with their work: "You all continue to do such an awesome job thinking about the importance of organizing an event sequence on effective narrative writing. I love the way you all thought about quotations from *Sideways Stories from Wayside School* that match up with our narrative sequence elements—both in our whole-class discussion and in small groups—and I was so impressed by your thoughts on the reflection questions!"

Recommendations for Teaching Students About Organizing an Event Sequence

In this section, I describe a step-by-step instructional process to use when helping students understand the narrative writing strategy of organizing an event sequence. The steps I recommend are:

1. Show students how published authors structure narrative sequences in their works.
2. Talk with students about why organizing an event sequence is an important component of effective narrative writing.

32 ◆ Narrative Writing Strategies

3. Have students analyze how published authors organize event sequences in their works.
4. Ask students to focus on organizing event sequences in their works.
5. Help students reflect on why organizing event sequences is important for their own narratives.

Each of these recommendations is described in detail in this section.

1. Show students how published authors structure narrative sequences in their works.

This initial step helps students learn the key aspects of narrative sequence while also allowing them to see what those aspects look like in action, enhancing students' understandings of this narrative writing tool, as well as their engagement in it. For instance, when introducing my fourth graders to this strategy, I explained the concepts of exposition, rising action, climax, falling action, and resolution to them, and paired these explanations with excerpts from Mary Pope Osborne's *Night of the Ninjas* that represent each of these narrative aspects. This instructional approach enabled me to provide my students with specific and concrete examples of the writing concepts I described. If I had simply explained the narrative sequence aspects without providing mentor examples from Osborne's work, the students would have likely had a harder time understanding the concepts. However, combining concept-specific instruction with mentor text examples of those writing strategies helped my students develop a strong understanding of this narrative writing tool.

2. Talk with students about why organizing an event sequence is an important component of effective narrative writing.

Once students understand the fundamentals of organizing an event sequence, I recommend focusing on why this concept is important to strong narrative writing. When doing this with my students, I highlight the following reasons why clear organization is significant to narrative writing:

1. It enables readers to understand the story clearly without confusion or frustration.
2. It makes the piece as engaging as possible because the story starts with the exposition and keeps the reader's interest through the rest of the narrative's sequence.

To help students grasp these ideas, I suggest showing them two documents: a table like the one depicted in Table 2.2 that lists the five key aspects of narrative sequence in order, along with quotations from an engaging, grade-level text that align with each of these concepts; and a table similar to the one in Table 2.3 that contains this same information, but out of its original order.

Showing students these two documents can help them grasp the significance of narrative sequence by allowing them to visualize how differently a narrative would look if it was presented out of its intended order. It can be difficult to conceptualize how a narrative would read if it began with its climax or resolution instead of its exposition, but this activity helps students see how this could look. When talking recently with my students about the importance of this writing strategy, I was excited that one of them commented on the benefits of looking at narrative aspects in their intended order, as well as out of order: "Seeing both of these really helps. I guess I always assumed writers wrote things however they wanted and never thought about why organizing things in order is important. Looking at these examples helped me see why organizing things in order is important."

3. Have students analyze how published authors organize event sequences in their works.

Next, I recommend releasing more responsibility to the students by asking them to analyze how published authors organize event sequences in their works, and to consider why the narrative sequence the author used was important to the effectiveness of the piece. Continuing the instructional process in this way not only gives students more ownership over their learning, but also gives you a chance to evaluate how well the students understand this writing strategy. In this activity (an example of which is described in this chapter's classroom snapshot), students work in groups or individually with a published text, to identify quotations from the text's exposition, rising action, climax, falling action, and resolution. Once the students have found these quotations, I suggest asking them to reflect on the question "Why is it important that the text you used followed this narrative sequence?" This question facilitates students' metacognitive thinking by asking them to consider further why the narrative writing tool of organizing an event sequence is important to effective writing.

As depicted in the classroom snapshot, I suggest guiding the whole class through this activity before asking students to work on it themselves, as this ensures the students' awareness of the procedures, and gives you a chance to emphasize any concepts you feel would benefit the students. Once you feel the class is ready, give each student or group a text to analyze, as well as the graphic organizer to complete (Table A2, Appendix A). While students work on the activity, I like to circulate the room and check in with them, especially because I do a lot of teaching when talking to the students while they work. For example, I recently met with a group of

34 ◆ Narrative Writing Strategies

fourth graders that were having a hard time identifying the rising action of their assigned story. These students and I had an excellent discussion about the features of expositions and rising actions, and the similarities and differences between them. This discussion alerted me to the students' misunderstandings and helped me clarify them. After this conversation, I was confident in their abilities to distinguish between these concepts and their understandings of the importance of both. The structure of this activity, and the increased ownership it placed on the students, helped make this conversation possible.

4. Ask students to focus on organizing event sequences in their works.

This step of the instructional process gives students even more responsibility by asking them to work on their own narratives and focus on the writing strategy of organizing event sequences while doing so. I prepare my students to do this by reminding them of the five key aspects of narrative sequence—exposition, rising action, climax, falling action, and resolution—and emphasizing that all of these components should be present in their pieces. I then ask the students to look at the narratives they've been working on and do the following:

1. identify any of these narrative sequence aspects that already exist in their works;
2. brainstorm some possibilities for how the other aspects might appear.

I then meet with the students individually, asking them to share their responses to these directions.

I recently conferred with the student who was working on the narrative about a Pittsburgh Steelers quarterback, described in Chapter 1, about the sequence of events in his narrative. He identified the piece's opening paragraph (see Figure 1.1) as representative of its exposition, explaining, "This first paragraph is definitely the exposition because it introduces Sam and says why playing QB for the Steelers is such a big deal to him." He then discussed how other aspects of the narrative's sequence of events might appear: "The next thing I'll work on will be the rising action, when Sam sees his long-lost brother, who ran away from home years ago after a fight, in the front row of the stands. This," the student continued, "will build up to the climax, when Sam scores a touchdown, realizes his brother is right in front of him, and has to decide what to do." This student continued to explain the narrative's falling action, in which Sam reaches into the stands to give his brother a football and hug him, and then the resolution, in which the two of them have dinner after the game. I left this conference thrilled with the student's understanding of how the key aspects of narrative sequence played a role in his story; I was very pleased with his acknowledgment of the piece's exposition, as well as his plan for continuing its sequence of events.

> **New Literacy Connection**
>
> A number of students with whom I have worked have remarked that they benefit from using multimedia graphic organizing tools, such as Microsoft Word's Smart Art, to organize the event sequence of their narratives. Doing so, some have explained to me, helps them visualize the events in their narratives and ensure that they have addressed each narrative sequence aspect. One student specifically identified as beneficial a Smart Art graphic that groups ideas in the shape of ordered, interconnected gears: "I had a gear for the exposition, a gear for the rising action, a gear for the climax, a gear for the falling action, a gear for the resolution. This made me be sure I had each of these things in my story and made me be sure I put them in order."

5. Help students reflect on why organizing event sequences is important to their own narratives.

This final step of the instructional process gives students an opportunity to further consider the significance of this writing tool for effective narratives. I have found that asking students to reflect on the importance of this strategy on their own writing further enhances the concept's relevance and applicability, as students must apply an analytical lens to the works that they themselves have created and/or planned. To help students reflect in this way, I recommend asking them the following questions:

1. "Why is it important that your narrative contains the key aspects of narrative sequence—exposition, rising action, climax, falling action, and resolution—and that presents them in an organized way?"
2. "How would your narrative be different if it didn't contain these narrative sequence aspects?"
3. "How would it be different if it didn't present them in an organized way?"

The student writing a narrative about a Pittsburgh Steelers quarterback reflected on these questions in ways that showed his understanding of the significance of organizing an event sequence; he responded to the first question by saying, "It's important that my story had those things so that it tells a full story. It would be weird and confusing if it didn't have a climax or a

36 ♦ Narrative Writing Strategies

resolution or something. It's important that they're organized so the story makes sense to people reading it." In response to the second and third questions, he explained that, without these components, the story "wouldn't be complete and it would be very confusing or uninteresting. People reading it would probably just get confused or frustrated and stop reading."

Final Thoughts on Organizing an Event Sequence

- ♦ The narrative writing strategy of organizing an event sequence is addressed in Common Core Writing Standards W.3.3.A, W.4.3.A, W.5.3.A, W.6.3.A, W.7.3.A, and W.8.3.A.
- ♦ Key aspects of narrative sequence, that authors must consider when organizing their works, are exposition, rising action, climax, falling action, and resolution.
- ♦ An effective narrative author will consider each of these narrative sequence aspects and structure the piece in a way that allows readers to clearly envision the order in which the story's key events take place.
- ♦ Two major reasons why organizing an event sequence is an important tool for a successful piece of narrative writing are:
  - ♦ If a narrative's events were disorganized, readers would not be able to determine when certain actions in the piece took place.
  - ♦ A narrative without an organized series of events would not be as interesting since the aspects of narrative sequence would not build on each other; for example, the exposition and rising action would no longer build up to the climax.
- ♦ When teaching students about organizing an event sequence:
  - ♦ show students how published authors structure narrative sequences in their works;
  - ♦ talk with students about why organizing an event sequence is an important component of effective narrative writing;
  - ♦ have students analyze how published authors organize event sequences in their works;
  - ♦ ask students to focus on organizing event sequences in their works;
  - ♦ help students reflect on why organizing event sequences is important to their own narratives.

3

Developing Experiences and Events

What Does "Developing Experiences and Events" Mean?

Think about a strong narrative you've read. Now, reflect back on the main experiences and events in that book; did the author briefly mention these experiences and events? Or did they develop them in great detail? Chances are that you answered "yes" to the second question. The Common Core State Writing Standards highlight the importance of developing experiences and events—Standards W.3.3.B, W.4.3.B, W.5.3.B, W.6.3.B, W.7.3.B, and W.8.3.B emphasize the significance of this concept. In this chapter, we'll explore: what "developing experiences and events" means; the importance of this writing tool to effective narrative writing; a description of a lesson on this concept; and five recommendations for helping your students develop experiences and events in their own works. In addition, we'll look at how published narrative writers apply this strategy to their works, and reflect on what makes those authors' pieces so effective.

First, let's think about what it means to develop experiences and events in a piece of narrative writing. Well-developed experiences and events are those that are discussed in detail and communicate their importance to the reader. Some ways writers develop experiences and events are through descriptions of the following components: the event's setting; a character's actions; a character's motivation; a conversation between characters; and a character's thoughts. Typically, authors include a number of these elements when discussing experiences and events in their works. For example, in the book *How to Eat Fried Worms*, author Thomas Rockwell uses all of the previously mentioned components—setting, actions, motivation, conversation, and thoughts—associated with an event to craft an in-depth description of it:

38 ♦ Narrative Writing Strategies

So Tom took Billy aside into a horse stall and put his arm around Billy's shoulder and talked to him about George Cunningham's brother's minibike, and how they could ride it on the trail under the power lines behind Odell's farm, up and down the hills, bounding over rocks, rhum-rhum. Sure it was a big worm, but it'd only be a couple more bites. Did he want to lose a minibike over *two bites?* Slop enough mustard and ketchup and horseradish on it and he wouldn't even taste it.

(Rockwell, 1973: p. 15)

This event takes place early in the book after Billy, who has taken a bet to eat fifteen worms in fifteen days, is reluctant to continue with his worm-eating challenge. Rockwell uses a great deal of detail to depict this conversation between Tom and Billy, highlighting Tom's statement that Billy should eat the worm in order to win a new minibike, and revealing the tactics Tom used to convey this message. This passage, which I've used with my students to illustrate this concept, is an excellent example of how a published writer develops a description of an event. In this chapter's next section, we'll explore why this writing strategy is so important to strong narrative writing.

Why Developing Experiences and Events Is Important to Effective Narrative Writing

Well-developed experiences and events are critical to effective narratives; through the use of this writing strategy, authors can discuss important events in depth, and communicate why they are important. It's important to note that authors don't have to discuss every event in a great deal of detail; rather, effective writers save especially detailed descriptions for experiences and events that have major impacts on their works. When I talk with my students about this concept, I explain that detailed event descriptions are best used strategically: "You don't want to discuss every single experience and event in your narrative in a whole bunch of detail," I tell them, "but you don't want to leave your readers without any in-depth information either. It's important to identify especially significant experiences and events and discuss them in detail."

To illustrate the importance of this strategy, let's think further about the previously discussed excerpt from *How to Eat Fried Worms*. In this passage, Thomas Rockwell describes Tom's conversation with Billy in detail, using this information to communicate why this event is important. Table 3.1 compares Rockwell's original description with a more bare-bones version of the same occurrence:

The lack of detail in the revised, less-developed version no longer clearly reveals the event's significance, while the original passage communicates

Developing Experiences and Events ◆ 39

Table 3.1 Detailed Description Compared with Revised, Concise Version

Original, Detailed Description	Revised, Concise Version
So Tom took Billy aside into a horse stall and put his arm around Billy's shoulder and talked to him about George Cunningham's brother's minibike, and how they could ride it on the trail under the power lines behind Odell's farm, up and down the hills, bounding over rocks, rhum-rhum. Sure it was a big worm, but it'd only be a couple more bites. Did he want to lose a minibike over *two bites?* Slop enough mustard and ketchup and horseradish on it and he wouldn't even taste it. (Rockwell, 1973: p. 15)	Tom talked to Billy about the minibike he could have if he just put some condiments on the worm and ate it.

to readers the excitement and possibilities associated with the minibike that Billy could possess if he conquers the worm challenge. The revised, less-developed version does not convey this same emotional tone. The matter-of-fact nature of the brief summary states the basic actions taking place, but does not allow readers to infer how much Tom and Billy would enjoy riding the minibike. This potential for enjoyment places an importance on the worm-eating challenge that the revised text does not illustrate.

So, why is developing experiences and events in detail important to effective narrative writing? As the comparison in Table 3.1 reveals, this writing tool allows authors to communicate the significance of certain meaningful events clearly and effectively. Elaborating on details such as actions, motivations, and conversations helps readers understand why particular situations are especially important. When working with your students on this concept, encourage them to think carefully about when to use a great deal of detail; successful published authors develop meaningful events and situations in their works, but they also summarize when necessary. The strongest authors save the most detailed descriptions for particularly significant events, as those are the ones that are most important for readers to understand clearly. In the next section, we'll take a look inside a fifth-grade classroom and examine how the students in that class worked to understand the importance of this writing strategy.

A Classroom Snapshot

"Today, we're going to be working more on the narrative-writing strategy of developing experiences and events," I tell my fifth graders. "I'd like to start our work today by making a comparison between this writing strategy and something else. How many of you watch sports?" I ask. The vast majority of students in the class raise their hands, to which I reply, "Okay, great. The narrative-writing tool of developing experiences and events is similar to something you may have noticed when watching sports."

A number of students in the class smile, appearing engaged, if a bit unsure of how I plan to connect these two entities. In our past few classes, these students and I have discussed the writing tool of developing experiences and events; we talked about what this strategy means and why it's important to effective writing. Today, the students are going to work in small groups to further develop their understanding of this concept. I introduce the day's work by presenting my sports comparison: "When you watch a sporting event on television and listen to the announcers, you may notice that the announcers describe certain events in a great deal of detail. What kind of events do they talk about in a lot of detail?"

"Real important ones," responds a student seated near the front of the room.

"That's right," I reply. "They don't go into detail about really unimportant events, like something that doesn't have much impact on the game's outcome. Instead, they really go into detail about events that are especially significant, such as a play that has a major effect on the result of the game. Announcers might describe a game-winning touchdown pass in a lot of detail because that's really important, but might just quickly summarize what isn't so important, like an incomplete pass early in the game."

I pause for a few seconds, noting the students in the class. To my delight, a number of them are nodding their heads, which suggests to me that they're grasping the comparison. Capitalizing on the students' apparent awareness of the connection I'm making, I recap my points and ask a probing question: "So, to summarize: sports announcers will often describe an event that's especially significant to the game's outcome in a lot of detail, but they'll usually provide just a brief summary of an event they don't see as really important to the game. Now, a question for you all: how can you compare these actions of sports announcers to the narrative-writing strategy of developing experiences and events?"

Several students raise their hands; I call on a student who states, "Sports announcers describe some events in detail just like narrative writers do."

"True," I reply. "What kind of events do they both describe in a lot of detail? Is it every single event?"

"No," answers another student. "They both go into detail about the most important [events]."

"Exactly," I respond. "In both situations—announcing sports or writing a narrative—people go into detail when describing an event that's especially important. Describing an event in detail helps people fully understand it and comprehend why it's important. If a sports announcer just briefly summarized a key play without explaining it and talking about why it's important, people watching the game might not understand why it's so important. The same is true for narrative writing: if a narrative writer describes an event in detail and explains why it's important, readers will understand its significance. If an author quickly summarizes a key event, readers won't understand the event and why it's so important."

Next, I introduce the day's activity, explaining to the students that in today's class they will work in groups and do the following:

1. Select a detailed, descriptive passage from *The Twits* by Roald Dahl (1980)—a novel the class has just finished reading—that describes an important event in the book.
2. Write down that passage on a handout I provide.
3. Turn the detailed, descriptive passage they just wrote down into a much more bare-bones version, and write the new version on the handout.
4. Reflect on why the author chose to write a detailed, descriptive version of the passage instead of a brief, less-developed version.

Table A3 (Appendix A) depicts the handout I give the students to complete during the activity (see Appendix A for a reproducible version of this handout that you can use with your students).

I divide the students into small groups of four or five, give each group a copy of the handout, and explain that I'll be checking in with them as they work: "I'm really excited to see your work on this activity. After everyone takes some time to get started, I'll come around and talk to each of you about your group's progress."

The students begin working, poring over their copies of *The Twits* and discussing the event descriptions that they'd like to use for this activity with one another. I sit down with a group and ask how they're doing: "Hey there! How are things going so far with your work?"

"Great," answers a student in the group. "We finished everything on the chart. We found a detailed description of an important event in *The Twits*, rewrote it in a much shorter way, and wrote about why we think the author described the event in detail."

"Wonderful!" I exclaim, thrilled by the group's progress. "Talk to me first about the detailed description of an important event that you identified."

"Okay. We picked out this paragraph here," a group member says, reading the following passage from *The Twits*, which describes Mr. Twit inflating balloons and tying them to his wife so that she floats away and is gone forever:

When that was done, he began filling the balloons with gas. Each balloon was on a long string and when it was filled with gas it pulled on its string, trying to go up and up. Mr. Twit tied the ends of the strings to the top half of Mrs. Twit's body. Some he tied around her neck, some under her arms, some to her wrists and some even to her hair.

(Dahl, 1980: p. 24)

42 ◆ Narrative Writing Strategies

"Very nice," I respond. "Now, let's hear your revised, less-developed version of this description."

"We turned it into, 'Mr. Twit filled up balloons with gas and tied them all over Mrs. Twit's body.'"

"Great job," I remark. "I really like the way you all put that event description into such simple terms. How about the response question on the third column of the handout? Why do you think Roald Dahl chose to write a detailed description of this event instead of a simple summary of it?"

Another student in the group answers: "The detailed description really helps you understand what happened because it shows you everything Mr. Twit did. I can picture what happened in my mind really clearly when I read the original description."

"Awesome," I praise the student's response. "Can you picture what took place when you read the revised, less detailed version?"

"Not really," says the student. "I mean, I know the basics, but I can't picture it nearly as well."

"Plus," interjects another student in the group, "all of these details show how important tying these balloons to Mrs. Twit is to Mr. Twit. We know everything he did, so we can see how important this was to him."

"Really nice work," I tell the students. "I love the way you all described how the information Roald Dahl included helps us readers visualize the event. I also love the way you discussed how this information reveals the importance of the event to Mr. Twit. I'm so proud of your fantastic work!"

I proceed to check in with the other groups, noting the passages they selected, the summarized versions they created, and the responses they formed. After I've spoken with all of the groups, I praise their work on the day's activity: "You all did really well today! I loved the way each group found detailed descriptions Roald Dahl used in *The Twits*, revised them, and analyzed why he chose to use these detailed descriptions in his book. This activity isn't easy because of everything you had to do on your own, but you all did great work!"

Recommendations for Teaching Students About Developing Experiences and Events

In this section, I describe a step-by-step instructional process to use when teaching students about the narrative-writing tool of developing experiences and events. The instructional steps I recommend are:

1. Show students detailed descriptions of experiences and events found in published texts.
2. Discuss with students why developing experiences and events is important for effective narrative writing.

Developing Experiences and Events ◆ 43

3. Have students analyze the significance of this writing strategy for published narratives.
4. Ask students to apply the writing tool of developing experiences and events to their own narratives.
5. Help students reflect on why developing significant experiences and events is important to their own narratives.

Each of these recommendations is described in detail in this section.

1. Show students detailed descriptions of experiences and events found in published texts.

Beginning this instructional process with published examples enhances students' understandings of what it means to develop experiences and events in depth. These models provide accessible touchstones for you and your students to use as you introduce this writing strategy to them and help them understand its fundamental attributes. When recently introducing this concept to my fifth graders, I showed them a number of published examples of detailed descriptions and events to develop their understandings of what this writing tool looks like in practice, such as the following excerpt from *The Phantom Tollbooth*:

Without stopping or looking up, Milo dashed past the buildings and busy shops that lined the street and in a few minutes reached home—dashed through the lobby—hopped onto the elevator— two, three, four, five, six, seven, eight, and off again—opened the apartment door—rushed into his room—flopped dejectedly into a chair, and grumbled softly, "Another long afternoon."

(Juster, 1961: p. 11)

While showing my students this example, I talked with them about all of the detail that author Norton Juster uses to describe Milo's experience going home and feeling unhappy while doing so. Juster uses specific imagery to help us envision the street on which Milo dashed, the particulars of his elevator ride, and the way he sat down in a chair. Sharing and discussing this example with my students helped them understand this writing strategy and prepared them well for the second part of this instructional process—exploring the concept's importance.

2. Discuss with students why developing experiences and events is important to effective narrative writing.

This step of the instructional process helps students understand why the writing concept of developing experiences and events in detail is an important tool for effective narrative writing. I recommend illustrating the

Table 3.2 Detailed Passage from *The Phantom Tollbooth* Compared with Revised, Concise Version

Original, Detailed Passage	Revised, Concise Version
Without stopping or looking up, Milo dashed past the buildings and busy shops that lined the street and in a few minutes reached home—dashed through the lobby—hopped onto the elevator—two, three, four, five, six, seven, eight, and off again—opened the apartment door—rushed into his room—flopped dejectedly into a chair, and grumbled softly, "Another long afternoon." (Juster, 1961: p. 11)	Milo quickly went home and unhappily sat down in a chair.

significance of this writing strategy by comparing detailed descriptions of events from published texts (such as the previously described excerpt from *The Phantom Tollbooth*) with revised, bare-bones versions of the same descriptions; the juxtaposition between the original, detailed passage and the new, much shorter version helps students understand why the detailed descriptions are so important to the success of the narrative.

For example, I recently highlighted the importance of this writing strategy by showing my students Table 3.2, which contains the passage from *The Phantom Tollbooth* described in the first recommendation alongside a less-developed version of the same paragraph:

After showing these passages to my students, I spoke with them about why the original, detailed passage is important to the narrative. In this conversation, we focused on how Juster's original text allows readers to envision the specifics of Milo's trip home, such as the "buildings and busy shops" he passed, and the way he "dashed through the lobby." In addition, the students and I discussed the language Juster uses to reveal Milo's feelings, highlighting actions such as "flopped dejectedly" and "grumbled softly." Without these details, I explained to my students, readers wouldn't be able to visualize Milo's commute or infer his feelings. Since Milo's unhappiness at this point in the narrative is important to the plot, it's especially significant that Juster helps readers clearly understand this situation.

New Literacy Connection

I've found that I can make my conversations with students about this writing strategy especially relevant by capitalizing on their knowledge of and interest in social media. In a recent conversation with a group of students, I explained that concise social-media postings (such as those one might write

Developing Experiences and Events ◆ 45

> on Facebook or Twitter) provide basic information about an event, but do not typically allow readers to develop in-depth understandings of it. In contrast, the detailed descriptions of key events found in effective narrative writing facilitate a thorough understanding of an event or experience. Highlighting the contrast between these two types of description can help students understand what well-developed experiences and events look like in narrative writing.

3. Have students analyze the significance of this writing strategy for published narratives.

Now that the students have considered what it means to develop experiences and events and have explored why it is important to effective writing, I recommend giving them more responsibility by asking them to work in small groups or individually, to analyze the significance of this strategy for published narratives. As described in this chapter's classroom snapshot, I like to conduct this activity by asking students to do the following:

◆ select a detailed passage from a published text that describes an important event in that book;
◆ write that passage on a handout I provide;
◆ create a simplified, less-developed version of the original passage and write that version on the handout;
◆ explain why they feel the author wrote a detailed, descriptive version of the passage instead of a concise version.

I suggest that students use a book that they've recently read for this activity so that they will be familiar with its details and events. As students work, I recommend conferring with each student or group (as I did in the classroom snapshot); this allows you to gauge students' understanding and provide individualized support. When I meet with students who are working on this activity, I pay special attention to their explanation of why the author chose to write a detailed description of the event instead of a concise one; I look for thoughtful analysis of how the detailed description helps readers visualize the event and grasp its significance. For example, the student group described in the classroom snapshot shared insight about both of these topics, commenting on how Roald Dahl's detailed discussion of Mr. Twit tying balloons to Mrs. Twit helped them "picture what happened" during this event, and "see how important [tying the balloons to Mrs. Twit] was to [Mr. Twit]."

4. Ask students to apply the writing tool of developing experiences and events to their own narratives.

46 ♦ Narrative Writing Strategies

This step of the instructional process gives students even more ownership of and responsibility for their learning. Before asking students to apply this writing strategy to their own narratives, I remind them that some key ways authors can develop experiences and events are through discussions of the event's setting, a character's actions, a character's motivation, a conversation between characters, and a character's thoughts. In addition, I reiterate to the students that authors do not describe all of the events in their narratives in great detail, focusing instead on the most important ones. When students work independently on applying this tool to their own pieces, I meet with them individually to assess their progress and provide guidance. When I confer with students, I ask the following questions: (1) What events have you described in detail? (2) What specific information have you included? and (3) Why are these events especially important to your narrative?

I asked these questions during a conference with the student who was writing the football-themed story I referred to in Chapters 1 and 2. He identified the following passage from his narrative, in which the protagonist sees his brother (to whom he hasn't spoken in years), as a detailed event description:

During our conversation this student explained, "One of the events I described in detail was the time when Sam saw his brother Jeff in the stands." He continued to say, "I included information about how hard Jeff was cheering for Sam, and exactly what he did while he was cheering, like where he was sitting, what he was wearing, and what he was holding. I figured this would really show what was going on and how excited Jeff was." Finally, the student commented on the event's importance, saying, "This is a really important event because it's the rising action in the story. It relates to the climax, when Sam ends up right in front of his brother."

5. Help students reflect on why developing significant experiences and events is important to their own narratives.

This final step of the instructional process helps students to fully understand the impact of the narrative-writing tool of developing experiences and events. To help students thoughtfully reflect on the importance of this strategy, I like to pose the following questions: (1) "Why is it important that you developed important experiences and events in your narrative?" and (2) "How would your narrative be different if you didn't develop these experiences and events in detail?" In a recent class discussion about these questions, a fifth grader writing a narrative about a girl who tries to protect the wildlife in her community explained, "It's very very important that I developed important experiences and events in my story because these are the things that the audience most needs to understand to really

Figure 3.1 Student Example of Detailed Event Description

Sam stood at the line of scrimmage and waited for all of the Steelers' offensive players to come out on the field so the play could begin. Sam looked at the fans in the stands and noticed one who was cheering especially hard for him. This fan was sitting in the front of row of the end zone stands, wearing a black and yellow jacket, and holding a "Go Sam!" sign in one hand and a yellow Steelers towel in another. Even though almost everyone at the game was cheering and waving a yellow towel, this person still stood out because of how loud he was screaming and how much he was waving his towel and sign. "That fan is really into the game," thought Sam. Then, when he looked closer, Sam noticed that this wasn't just any fan: it was his long-lost brother Jeff! Sam and Jeff hadn't seen each other since five years ago, when Jeff ran away from home after an awful fight with Sam and his dad. Both Sam and his dad tried to get Jeff to work harder in school, but Jeff got upset by their suggestions and ran away.

get what's going on. Like when Marissa [the book's protagonist] meets with the Governor to try to get him to protect the animals she wants him to protect, it's really important that readers understand what's happening there and why it's important." This student continued to explain how her work would be different if key experiences and events were not developed in depth: "If I didn't do that, it would be much harder for the audience to really understand important events. They might know the main things that happened, like Marissa met with the Governor, but wouldn't understand them in real detail."

Final Thoughts on Developing Experiences and Events

♦ The narrative-writing strategy of developing experiences and events is addressed in Common Core Writing Standards W.3.3.B, W.4.3.B, W.5.3.B, W.6.3.B, W.7.3.B, and W.8.3.B.

♦ Well-developed experiences and events are those that are discussed in detail and communicate their importance to the reader.

♦ Some ways writers develop experiences and events are through descriptions of the following components: the event's setting, a character's actions, a character's motivation, a conversation between characters, and a character's thoughts.

♦ The writing strategy of developing experiences and events in detail is important to effective narrative writing because it enables authors to discuss important events in depth, and communicate why they are important.

♦ Authors don't have to discuss every event in a great deal of detail; rather, effective writers save especially detailed descriptions for experiences and events that have major impacts on their works.

♦ When teaching students about developing experiences and events:
  ♦ show students detailed descriptions of experiences and events found in published texts;
  ♦ discuss with students why developing experiences and events is important to effective narrative writing;
  ♦ have students analyze the significance of this writing strategy for published narratives;
  ♦ ask students to apply the writing tool of developing experiences and events to their own narratives;
  ♦ help students reflect on why developing significant experiences and events is important to their own narratives.

4

Incorporating Characterization

What Does "Incorporating Characterization" Mean?

A strong narrative does more than tell a story: it also enables readers to understand the emotions, personalities, and attributes of its characters. This writing strategy, often referred to as characterization, is identified in Common Core State Writing Standards W.3.3.B, W.4.3.B, W.5.3.B, W.6.3.B, W.7.3.B, and W.8.3.B as an important component of narrative writing. In this chapter, we'll examine the following: what "incorporating characterization" means; why it is important to effective narrative writing; a description of a lesson on this writing strategy; and recommendations for helping your students incorporate characterization into their own writings. We'll also explore published examples of characterization, and discuss what the authors of those works do to make their passages effective.

Writers incorporate characterization into their works by revealing important information about their characters. The most effective authors often convey these points through behaviors, such as actions, thoughts, and dialogue, and allow readers to infer those characteristics. For example, instead of saying "this person is angry," an author may describe a character stomping their feet, yelling, or balling up their fist to enable readers to infer this anger. Jack Gantos' novel *I am Not Joey Pigza* contains an excellent example of an author using a character's actions to allow readers to make inferences about that individual: instead of saying, "Joey's father really loves Joey's mother," Gantos describes actions performed by Joey's father that convey this emotion:

♦ 49

And then he stood on a chair and gave an amazing speech about how Mom was the greatest woman in the world, with the most forgiving heart and the most angelic face, and that he was the luckiest man on the planet.

(Gantos, 2007: p. 51)

Another effective example of characterization is found in Kashmira Sheth's (2004) book *Blue Jasmine*. Sheth characterizes the book's main character, Seema Trivedi, as feeling very nervous when she answers a math problem in school. However, Sheth does not simply have Seema say, "I was nervous"; instead, she uses specific descriptions of Seema's actions to enable readers to infer this: "I got up. My hand was shaking as I wrote on the blackboard. Between me and the blackboard was my warm breath, which made me break out in a sweat" (p. 52). Both this excerpt from *Blue Jasmine* and the previously described example from *I am Not Joey Pigza* effectively illustrate characterization, as they use descriptions of characters to convey their emotions, personalities, and attributes to readers.

Why Incorporating Characterization Is Important to Effective Narrative Writing

Strong characterization is an important component of effective narrative writing; it reveals information about characters and does so in engaging ways that keep readers' attention. When I discuss the importance of this concept with my students, I address each of the ways characterization enhances a narrative. I start by explaining that the writing tool of characterization allows readers to develop strong understandings of characters. "Without characterization," I recently told a class of fifth graders, "we wouldn't know important information about our characters, like their feelings, beliefs, interests, and backgrounds. A story would be far less interesting if we didn't know anything about the characters. It would still have a plot, but the actions in that plot would be done by people we wouldn't know anything about." I continued to share with these students how characterization tactics that authors use can engage readers: "So, we know that stories are more interesting if we know about the characters, but it's also important to know that there are certain ways authors describe their characters to make their narratives especially interesting. It wouldn't be very interesting if an author just said, "This character is nice" or "This one is mean." It's a lot more fun to read a story that *shows* what a character is like through actions, conversations, and thoughts than to read one that just *tells* what a character is like. I know that I wouldn't be as interested in a story in which the author just told me all the characters' personalities as I would be in one where the author showed these personalities."

"You mean like making a character do brave things instead of just saying a character is brave?" asked a student.

"Exactly," I responded. "It's much more interesting to read about the brave things a character does than to just read a statement that a character is brave."

Let's explore the importance of this writing strategy further by taking a look at a published example of characterization in Carl Hiaasen's novel *Flush*. In this novel, the protagonist Noah Underwood characterizes two boys, named Jasper Jr. and Bull, as bullies. However, Hiaasen doesn't simply have Noah say "Jasper Jr. and Bull bullied me"; he uses events in Noah's narration to show it, using passages like the following one to convey information about characters:

> But Jasper Jr. didn't hit me again. Instead he spit in my face, which was worse in a way.
>
> He forced a laugh and called me a couple of dirty names and headed back toward the johnboat. He was shaking that hand he'd hit me with, as if there was a crab or a mousetrap attached to it. Bull was following behind, cackling like a hyena.
>
> (Hiaasen, 2005: p. 38)

In this passage, Hiaasen—through Noah's description—uses Jasper Jr. and Bull's actions to depict their personalities, noting that Jasper Jr. hit Noah, spat in his face, and called him names, while Bull laughed at the situation. This example of characterization illustrates the importance of this concept to effective narrative writing—it reveals characters' attributes (in this case, Jasper Jr. and Bull's identities as bullies) and does so through engaging descriptions of actions that keep readers interested. If Hiaasen did not use such effective characterization, readers would either not know these characters' personalities, or would learn of them in a much less engaging way (such as telling readers these attributes rather than showing them). In the next section, we'll take a look inside a fifth-grade classroom and examine how the students in that class develop their understandings of characterization.

A Classroom Snapshot

I begin today's class on characterization by asking my fifth graders what has struck them about this concept so far: "We've been talking about characterization a lot this week. What are some things you've noticed from our conversations?"

"Characterization tells you about the characters," one student answers. "It lets you know their personalities and things like that."

"Absolutely," I say to the student. "That's an important part of characterization. What else have you all noticed about our conversations on this topic?"

52 ♦ Narrative Writing Strategies

"It makes a story a whole lot more interesting," another responds, "because it shows what a character is like, instead of telling what he or she's like."

"Nice job," I reply. "Showing a character's personality, background, and emotions through their actions rather than just telling us about those things makes a narrative much more interesting to read. Today, we're going to continue to explore the writing tool of characterization. We're going to get into groups, like we've done before, and I'm going to ask each group to do the following: select a book from our classroom library (or use a book you're reading right now for independent reading); find an example of characterization in that book; and use that example of characterization to complete the chart that I'll give each group."

I then place the chart depicted in Table A4 (Appendix A) on the document camera, and explain its components to the students. (A reproducible version of this chart that you can use with your students can be found in Appendix A.)

"This chart asks you to first write down a strong example of characterization from a published text that shows readers something about a character instead of telling them. Then, it asks you to take that passage and revise it so that it tells us about the character instead of showing us. Finally, the chart asks you to reflect on why it's important that the original passage shows us about the character instead of telling us. I'm really excited to see what you all come up with, but first, we're going to talk through an example together.

"I'm going to share with all of you a passage from one of my favorite books that I think does a great job of showing instead of telling. It's from a book called *From the Mixed-Up Files of Mrs. Basil E. Frankweiler* by E.L. Konigsburg." I place the opening paragraph of the book on the document camera:

> Claudia knew that she could never pull off the old-fashioned kind of running away. That is, running away in the heat of anger with a knapsack on her back. She didn't like discomfort; even picnics were untidy and inconvenient: all those insects and the sun melting the ice on the cupcakes. Therefore, she decided that her leaving home would not be just running from somewhere but would be running to somewhere. To a large place, a comfortable place, an indoor place, and preferably a beautiful place. And that's why she decided upon the Metropolitan Museum of Art in New York City.
>
> (Konigsburg, 1967: p. 5)

"This passage shows instead of tells," I think aloud to the students, "because of all the descriptive language and detail it uses to convey to us that Claudia lives a privileged life. Now, let's use this passage to complete a chart like the one you'll use in your group work activities."

I place the chart depicted in Table A4 (Appendix A) on the document camera and begin by telling the students, "The first thing this chart asks for is the original passage that shows the character's attributes, so I'm going to write the excerpt we just looked at together right here." After I write the previously described passage from on the chart, I continue, "The next thing the chart asks for is a revised version of the text that tells instead of shows. So, instead of using all of the great characterization that author E.L. Konigsburg uses in the original passage, we're going to revise the passage so that it tells the reader about Claudia instead of showing it. In this section of the chart, I'm going to write, 'Claudia is privileged and accustomed to the finer things in life; these personality traits played major roles in her choice to run away to the Metropolitan Museum of Art in New York City.' Do you all think that information tells readers about Claudia instead of showing them?"

"Yeah," responds a student. "It just says what Claudia is like. In the first one, the author shows what Claudia's like by describing her likes and dislikes."

"Good," I reply. "The original passage doesn't come out and say, 'Claudia is privileged.' Instead, it allows readers to infer that message through the description of the things Claudia doesn't enjoy. Now, let's take a look at the third column on this chart, which asks why it's important that the original passage shows instead of tells. What are some reasons that it's important that it does this?"

I call on a student in the front of the room who explains, "[Showing instead of telling] lets us know the character's personality."

"That's right," I affirm. "The original passage really shows us Claudia's personality. I feel that I have a strong sense of her as a person after reading it. I'll write 'Shows character's personality' in the third column. Can anyone think of any other reasons why it's important that the original passage shows instead of tells?"

"I think," answers another student in the class, "that it's important because it gives a lot of detail. The example that tells doesn't give much detail."

"Nicely said," I reply. "The details in the original passage are definitely important. They make the piece a lot more interesting than the telling version, which doesn't use these details. Using specific details like the ones can make a piece much more engaging and fun to read. I'm going to write 'More specific details, which make the passage more interesting' in the third column."

I praise the students on their responses and explain that the next step is for them to work in small groups on this activity. I give each group of students a copy of the handout and ask them to look through the books from the classroom library or those they're using for independent reading for a strong example of characterization that they can use for this activity. The students take several minutes to select books and look through them to find passages that effectively describe characters using the "showing, not telling" strategy. Once they've begun to find and discuss examples, I begin to move around the room and check in with the student groups.

54 ♦ Narrative Writing Strategies

One group with which I confer is working with the book *Diary of a Wimpy Kid: Hard Luck* by Jeff Kinney (2013). I begin my conversation with them by noting the text they've selected: "I love that book!"

"I love it too!" responds a student in the group. "And we like the characterization in it also."

"Fantastic!" I reply. "Talk to me about what you noticed. What passage did you pick out that shows instead of tells about a character?"

"We found this one that shows that Greg is jealous about how Rowley's a lot more focused on his girlfriend than he is on Greg." She proceeds to read aloud the following passage from *Diary of a Wimpy Kid: Hard Luck*:

Wherever Rowley is, his girlfriend Abigail is, too. And even if she ISN'T there, it SEEMS like she is. I invited Rowley to my house for a sleepover last weekend so the two of us could spend some time together, but after about two hours I gave up trying to have any fun.
(Kinney, 2013: p. 4)

"Nice job, you all, of finding this passage that, as you said, show's Greg's feelings. How did you turn it into a version that tells instead of shows?"

"We changed it to, 'I'm jealous because Rowley's always focused on his girlfriend,'" answers another student in the group.

"Great work," I reply. "I really like that version. It's very to the point and definitely tells us Greg's feelings instead of showing us. Now for the final point to consider: why is it important that the original passage shows instead of tells?"

"I think," explains a group member, "it's because the original one is so specific. It says exactly what Rowley does and shows how he focuses on Abigail."

"Yeah," interjects another student. "Plus, the first version shows why Greg's jealous—because either Abigail is with Rowley, or Rowley isn't any fun when she isn't with him."

"Really nicely said," I respond. "So, if I heard you correctly: it's important that the original passage shows instead of tells because the original one is so specific and shows exactly why Greg's jealous."

"And," says another student, "it's just much more fun to read. The examples are much more fun to read about than Greg just saying, 'I'm jealous.'"

Recommendations for Teaching Students About Incorporating Characterization

In this section, I describe a step-by-step instructional process to use when teaching students about incorporating characterization in narrative writing. The instructional steps I recommend are:

1. Show students effective examples of characterization drawn from published texts.

Incorporating Characterization ♦ 55

2. Discuss with students why strong characterization is important to narrative writing.
3. Ask students to find and analyze examples of characterization in published texts.
4. Work with students as they apply the writing tool of characterization to their own works.
5. Help students reflect on why the effective use of characterization is important to their own narratives.

Each of these recommendations is described in detail in this section.

1. Show students effective examples of characterization drawn from published texts.

Beginning this instructional process by sharing published examples of effective characterization with your students provides them with concrete examples of this writing strategy. When presenting these examples to your students, I recommend highlighting how published authors show their characters' personalities to readers instead of telling them, noting that some of the most frequently used characterization methods are descriptions of characters' actions, thoughts, and dialogue. For example, I recently shared the previously described excerpt from *Blue Jasmine* with my fifth graders, noting how author Kashmira Sheth uses specific descriptions of a character's actions to convey to readers that the character is nervous. To do so, I placed the passage—which reads, "I got up. My hand was shaking as I wrote on the blackboard. Between me and the blackboard was my warm breath, which made me break out in a sweat" (p. 52)—on the document camera, and identified all of the actions that illustrated the character's nervousness. After this, I explained to the students, "This is what really effective characterization looks like—descriptions of a character's actions, thoughts, and/or words that show something about the character to readers."

2. Discuss with students why strong characterization is important to narrative writing.

Once you've shown your students examples of effective characterization, I recommend talking with them about why characterization is an important aspect of effective narrative writing. When I discuss the importance of this concept with my students, I explain that strong characterization is important because it informs readers of characters' attributes, personalities, and emotions, and does so in interesting ways. While a piece of writing that tells readers of a character's personality instead of showing them can still give basic information about that character, I tell my students it does not do so in a particularly engaging way. To illustrate this concept, I'll show students an example of strong characterization from a published text and then compare that with a revised version of the example that tells readers about a character instead of showing them. This helps students see

56 ♦ Narrative Writing Strategies

the difference between strong and weak characterization, and to understand the importance of this concept to narrative writing.

In a recent conversation with students about this topic, I showed them the following excerpt from Sharon Creech's book *Pleasing the Ghost*, which describes a dog named Bo's excitement in a clear and engaging way:

> Bo bounded down the stairs, out the door, and stopped at the curb, wagging his tail. I led him across the street, and he leaped toward Uncle Arvie, barking and wiggling his back end. He tumbled right through Uncle Arvie and collapsed on the ground. "Yip!" he squeaked
> (Creech, 1996: p. 18).

After reading this example with my students, I pointed out that this description not only reveals Bo's excitement about seeing Uncle Arvie, but also uses specific and powerful action words that convey this excitement. "If this passage just said, 'Bo was excited to see Uncle Arvie,' it would be a lot less interesting and a lot less specific. The vivid action words here show us what Bo is feeling and do so in a really engaging, fun-to-read way."

3. Ask students to find and analyze examples of characterization in published texts.

At this point in the instructional process, I recommend giving more responsibility to the students by asking them to work in small groups or individually to find and analyze strong examples of characterization in published works. I ask students to analyze the examples they find by writing down the original example of characterization that shows instead of tells, writing a revised version of that passage that tells instead of shows, and then reflecting on why it's important that the original passage shows readers the character's attributes instead of telling them.

I recommend beginning the activity by modeling it for the students. In this chapter's classroom snapshot, I describe how I modeled this task; I began by showing students a passage from the book *From the Mixed-Up Files of Mrs. Basil E. Frankweiler* that characterizes a young lady named Claudia as privileged and accustomed to the finer things in life. After sharing this passage, I changed it to a new version designed to tell instead of show. Finally, I talked with the students about why it's important that the original author showed us about Claudia's personality instead of telling us. Once you've demonstrated to your students how to do this, give each group or individual (depending on how you choose to construct the activity) the graphic organizer depicted in Table A4 (Appendix A) and ask them to select a book to use for the activity. While your students work on this task, meet with them to gauge their progress and provide them with any needed support. Once you're satisfied with your students' identification and analysis of characterization, you can move to the next step in this instructional process, in which students apply this strategy to their own works.

4. Work with students as they apply the writing tool of characterization to their own works.

This next step gives students even more ownership of their learning, as it calls for them to put the writing strategy of characterization into practice in their own narratives. I explain to my students there are two ways for them to apply this tool to their works. The first is to review previous examples of characterization in their pieces, examine them to see if they meet the standards of strong characterization we've been discussing, and make any revisions needed. The second is for the students to continue to write their existing narratives and be sure to show readers what characters are like through descriptions of their actions, thoughts, and dialogue.

While the students work independently on applying this writing tool to their works, I suggest holding one-on-one conferences with them. In these conferences, I ask students to identify strong examples of characterization in their narratives and then explain to me why those excerpts represent effective characterization. The students' identification and explanation of these examples allows me to determine how strong their understanding of this concept is, and indicates if I need to provide extra support to any students. I recently conferred with a student who explained that, after learning about characterization, she made a number of revisions to her narrative when examining it with this concept in mind: "When I [reviewed my narrative with characterization in mind], I found some places where I can show more instead of tell. I'm writing about a girl who loves horses. I found places where I can show [with her actions] how she loves her horse instead of just saying that she loves her horse."

New Literacy Connection

Students can also use forms of multimedia to complement their written descriptions of characters. I recently worked with a student who was writing a narrative about an aspiring rapper. This student explained that she included audio files of music that was important to the main character: "Kayshawna [the story's protagonist] is really influenced by [late rapper] 2Pac's music. I explained this in the story, but I also put in some links to some 2Pac songs so people reading can listen to them and be more familiar with 2Pac." This student explained that, since 2Pac's music is so important to the main character "putting in links to these songs is important because the songs can help readers understand her."

5. Help students reflect on why the effective use of characterization is important to their own narratives.

Asking students to reflect on how this strategy enhances their works helps them further grasp its utility as a writing tool by prompting them to think in depth about how strong characterization maximizes the effectiveness of their narratives. To help students reflect, I recommend posing the following questions: (1) "Why is it important that you used the writing strategy of characterization effectively in your narrative?" and (2) "What would your narrative be like if you did not use this strategy effectively?" The student discussed in the previous recommendation, who was working on a piece about a horse enthusiast, explained: "Characterization made my story a lot better, especially showing instead of telling. It showed readers that the character in my story loves horses, but did it with her actions, which is much more interesting [than simply telling readers]." This student continued to reflect on what her narrative would be like without effective characterization, "If I didn't describe my character by showing instead of telling, the story wouldn't have as much as action and would be a lot more boring. It was like that at first, but once I worked on the characterization, I think the story got a lot better."

Final Thoughts on Incorporating Characterization

- Incorporating characterization is addressed in Common Core State Writing Standards W.3.3.B, W.4.3.B, W.5.3.B, W.6.3.B, W.7.3.B, and W.8.3.B.
- Writers incorporate characterization into their works by revealing important information about their characters.
- The most effective authors often convey information about characters through behaviors such as actions, thoughts, and dialogue, and expect readers to infer those characteristics.
    - This is often called "showing, not telling" because authors are showing readers that a character possesses a certain characteristic rather than simply stating information such as "this person is nice," or "this person is mean."
- Effective characterization is important to strong narrative writing for two key reasons:
    - It reveals important information about characters.
    - It does so in engaging ways that keep readers' attention.
- When teaching students about incorporating characterization:
    - show students effective examples of characterization drawn from published texts;
    - discuss with students why strong characterization is important to narrative writing;
    - ask students to find and analyze examples of characterization in published texts;
    - work with students as they apply the writing tool of characterization to their own works;
    - help students reflect on why the effective use of characterization is important to their own narratives.

5

Including Transitional Language

What Does "Including Transitional Language" Mean?

Think back to a time when you've told or written a story: you probably didn't simply list a serious of disconnected actions with no transitions between them. Instead, you likely used "transitional language"; words and phrases that establish a connection or relationship between events and ideas. The Common Core State Writing Standards emphasize the importance of this concept to narrative writing, and Standards W.3.3.C, W.4.3.C, W.5.3.C, W.6.3.C, W.7.3.C, and W.8.3.C highlight its significance. In this chapter, we'll investigate the following: what "including transitional language" means; why this concept is important to effective narrative writing; a description of a lesson on this writing tool; and key recommendations for helping your students include transitional language in their own narratives. While doing so, we'll examine how published authors incorporate transitional language into their works, and explore what makes their uses of this concept so effective.

Let's get started by exploring further what this writing strategy is. Just as writers use some types of language to start a story in an engaging way and other types to accurately describe a character, they use specific kinds of words and phrases—called transitional language—to establish relationships between ideas and events. Transitional language is especially common in narrative writing because of all of the actions, settings, and characters that are found in works of this genre. Figure 5.1 lists some transitional words and phrases that are widely used in narrative writing.

It's important to note that transitional language doesn't just link ideas and events that are similar; writers also use transitional language when the ideas in statements differ. For example, a writer might use the term

♦ 59

60 ♦ Narrative Writing Strategies

Figure 5.1 Some Widely Used Transitional Words and Phrases

Also
However
But
Meanwhile
Instead
Fortunately
Unfortunately
Afterwards
Then
Next
Later
Finally
In addition
In contrast
For example
Despite this
At the same time

"however" to transition between two different events, and the phrase "in addition" to move between two similar ones. Whether connecting statements that resemble one another or ideas that differ greatly, narrative writers frequently incorporate the writing tool of transitional language.

Why Including Transitional Language Is Important to Effective Narrative Writing

Transitional language is important to strong narrative writing because it increases the sense of flow in a piece of writing, and clearly communicates how two events and ideas relate to each other. Without this writing tool, a narrative would feel disjointed and would not directly convey to readers how aspects of the piece are similar or different. To illustrate the importance of this concept, let's take a look at the following example from Frank Cottrell Boyce's (2004) novel *Millions*, in which Damian, the book's narrator and protagonist, uses the word "then" to establish a connection

Including Transitional Language ◆ 61

Table 5.1 Example 1: Comparison of Published Text with and without Transitional Language

Original Text	Text without Transitional Language	Why the Transitional Language Is Important to the Original Passage
"Mr. Quinn came over and touched my shoulder. Then he leaned down and whispered to me to come with him." (Boyce, 2004: p. 21)	"Mr. Quinn came over and touched my shoulder. He leaned down and whispered to me to come with him."	The word "then" enhances the flow of the narration and clearly communicates the order of events in the passage.

between two events: "Mr. Quinn came over and touched my shoulder. Then he leaned down and whispered to me to come with him" (p. 21). The use of "then" ensures a smooth narration; without it, this event description would not flow nearly as well. In addition, this word clearly portrays the order of events, indicating that Mr. Quinn leaned down and whispered to Damian *after* touching his shoulder. Table 5.1 compares the original text of this passage with how it would look without the transitional word "then," and describes the significance of this transitional language.

Boyce also uses transitional language at other points in *Millions,* such as at the opening of the narrative, in which he has Damian use the transitional word "but" to distinguish between Damian's narration style and his brother Anthony's:

> If Anthony was telling this story, he'd start with the money. It always comes down to money, he says, so you might as well start there. He'd probably put, "Once upon a time there were 229,370 little pounds sterling," and go on until he got to, "and they all lived happily ever after in a high-interest bank account." But he's not telling this story. I am.
>
> (Boyce, 2004: p. 1)

Without the word "but," it would be much harder for readers to make sense of this passage. This word is used to indicate a shift in the information the piece conveys by transitioning from what the story would be like if Anthony told it to how Damian will tell it. As currently constructed, the passage relies on the word "but" to help signal that Damian is the narrator, not Anthony, and that the kind of information Damian will share will vary from the type Anthony would have communicated. Table 5.2 compares the original version of this opening section of *Millions* with how it would read without the transitional word "but," and then discusses the significance of this term.

As these excerpts from *Millions* show, transitional language is an important tool for effective narrative writing. This writing strategy enables

62 ♦ Narrative Writing Strategies

Table 5.2 Example 2: Comparison of Published Text with and without Transitional Language

Original Text	Text without Transitional Language	Why the Transitional Language Is Important to the Original Passage
If Anthony was telling this story, he'd start with the money. It always comes down to money, he says, so you might as well start there. He'd probably put, "Once upon a time there were 229,370 little pounds sterling," and go on until he got to, "and they all lived happily ever after in a high-interest bank account." But he's not telling this story. I am. (Boyce, 2004: p. 1)	If Anthony was telling this story, he'd start with the money. It always comes down to money, he says, so you might as well start there. He'd probably put, "Once upon a time there were 229,370 little pounds sterling," and go on until he got to, "and they all lived happily ever after in a high-interest bank account." He's not telling this story. I am.	The transitional word "but" helps readers understand this passage; it indicates that Anthony is not narrating the story and conveys that the kind of information Anthony would have communicated differs from the type Damian (the actual narrator) will discuss.

authors to enhance the clarity of a narrative by establishing relationships between pieces of information, maximizing a piece's sense of flow, and illustrating the order in which events occur. In the next section, we'll take a look inside a sixth-grade classroom and examine how the students in that class apply their knowledge of this concept.

A Classroom Snapshot

"I want to begin class today," I tell my sixth graders, "by praising you all on how well you did in our last class when we discussed the importance of transitional language. You all were really active in our discussions and shared great ideas." I pause to see many of the students smiling at these compliments and then continue: "Today, we're going to work on a similar idea—the importance of transitional language in narrative writing—but, this time, you're going to be more in charge. And middle schoolers like to be in charge, right?" I add jokingly.

"How are we going to be in charge?" asks a young man sitting in the front of the room.

"Great question," I respond. "Well, remember how last time I showed you some published passages that contain transitional language, then showed you how those passages would look without transitional language,

Including Transitional Language ♦ 63

and after that we talked together about why the transitional language is important to the original passage?"

The students nod their heads and I continue: "Well, our activity is similar to that one, but you'll be the ones finding the original published passage, rewriting it without transitional language, and then analyzing the importance of the author's use of transitional language. This will be more difficult than our last activity because you'll need to keep a careful eye out for examples of transitional language as you look through published books. Remember all of the transitional words and phrases we've discussed—and especially remember that transitional language can link ideas that are similar as well as those that are different."

I remind the students of some of the high-frequency words and phrases we've discussed (such as those in Figure 5.1) and get the activity started. I begin by dividing the class of twenty students into five groups of four, and then give each group the handout depicted in Table A5. (This handout, a version of the chart depicted in Tables 5.1 and 5.2, is available in Appendix A for you to copy and use with your students.)

"For this activity," I explain, "the book you use is up to you and your group members. You can look through your independent reading books, as well as those in our classroom library. I'll give everyone some time to get started on looking through these books and finding passages that contain transitional language. After a few minutes have passed, I'll start conferring with all of the groups."

The students comb through books, identifying examples of transitional language and sharing them with their group members. Thrilled by the enthusiasm with which the students are approaching the task, I say, "I'm so happy to see your hard work so far. I can't wait to hear what all of you find."

Several minutes later, I begin to confer with the small groups, first sitting down with a group using the book *Escape from Mr. Lemoncello's Library* (Grabenstein, 2013).

"Hey, everyone," I greet the students. "You all seem like you've made great progress."

"Yeah," responds a student in the group. "We found a lot of transitional language in this book."

"Fantastic!" I reply. "Tell me which passage containing transitional language you decided to use for the activity."

"We picked this one right here," answers a student, reading the following passage out loud:

For this assembly, the seventh graders, most of whom were twelve years old, were told to sit in the front rows, close to the stage. That made Kyle feel a little better. At least he'd get a chance to see Mr. Lemoncello up close and personal. But his hero wasn't even onstage.

(Grabenstein, 2013: p. 32f.)

64 ♦ Narrative Writing Strategies

"Nice job," I tell the student. "Now, tell me what transitional language you noticed and how the passage reads without it."

"The transitional word here is 'but,'" responds another student. "Without it, most [of the passage] would be the same, but the last sentence would be different. It would say 'His hero wasn't even onstage' instead of 'But his hero wasn't even onstage.'"

"Very well said," I reply. "Now, let's think about the last column of the handout that asks why the transitional language is important to the passage. Why do you all think the transitional word 'but' is important here?"

"It's important," answers a group member, "because of how much it makes the book easier to read. Try reading it without that word: it's much harder to read. It definitely doesn't have a good flow."

"And," interjects another student, "the word 'but' shows that something different is going to happen. Like, I might say, 'I was going to go swimming, but I forgot my bathing suit.' This example is like that too. We think Kyle's going see Mr. Lemoncello on stage, but then Mr. Lemoncello isn't there."

"Outstanding explanations!" I exclaim. "I love the points you made—this transitional word definitely makes the passage easier to read and clearly indicates that the events of the story are going to shift in some way from what's expected. Fantastic work on this activity!"

Recommendations for Teaching Students About Including Transitional Language

In this section, I describe a step-by-step instructional process for teaching students about the writing strategy of including transitional language in narrative writing. The steps I recommend are:

1. Show students examples of published texts that incorporate transitional language.
2. Discuss with students why transitional language is an important concept to effective narrative writing.
3. Ask students to identify transitional language in published writing and analyze its significance.
4. Have students apply the writing strategy of using transitional language to their own narratives.
5. Help students reflect on the importance of transitional language to their own works.

Each of these recommendations is described in detail in this section.

1. Show students examples of published texts that incorporate transitional language.

Showing students published examples of transitional language provides an excellent point of entry into this topic. When I do this with my students, I begin by placing a published sentence on the document camera that contains transitional language. Next, I identify any transitional words or phrases in the sentence, and explain that the text I've pointed out is an example of transitional language, which I describe to the students as words and phrases that establish a connection or relationship between events and ideas. I then show my students a list of high-frequency transitional words and phrases (see Figure 5.1).

When showing published transitional language to your students, I recommend displaying examples that link similar ideas, as well as those that connect different ones; this helps students understand that authors use transitional words and phrases to connect both kinds of statements. In a recent conversation on this topic with a group of sixth graders, I showed the students the excerpts from the novel *Millions,* discussed earlier in this chapter. Since one of these excerpts uses the transitional word "then" to connect similar pieces of information and the other uses the word "but" to link differing statements, these selections provide examples of different uses of transitional language. Some of my students commented that they were surprised that transitional words and phrases link both kinds of information: one shared, "When you started talking about transitional words, I was like, 'Oh, I know what this is,' but I never thought about connecting different things with these kinds of words."

2. Discuss with students why transitional language is an important concept to effective narrative writing.

Once you've shown your students published examples of transitional language, I recommend delving more deeply into the significance of the concept by talking with them about why this is a tool writers use to create strong narratives. To facilitate these conversations, I take the published examples I showed my students in the first step of this instructional process, and pair them with revised versions of those examples that no longer contain the transitional language. For example, when conducting this activity recently with my sixth graders, I took the two previously described examples from *Millions* and presented each one to the students without its transitional language. The juxtaposition of the original text and the revised version with no transitional words or phrases helped students to see the differences in the passages.

After you show the original and revised passages to your students, lead them in a discussion of why the transitional language is important to the original passage. Some questions I like to pose in these discussions are: "What is the original passage like without its transitional language?" and "What impact does the lack of transitional language have on us as readers?" By responding to these questions, students consider the usefulness of this concept for effective writing and think metacognitively about its importance. In a recent discussion with my sixth graders about the use of the transitional word "then," in an excerpt from *Millions*, a number of students demonstrated their ability to think critically about the importance of this term. One explained, "The word 'then' doesn't normally seem that important to me, but it's really important [to this passage]. When you take it out, everything seems weird and things don't sound right." Another student shared, "When you don't use [transitional] words like 'then,' there's just no connection between ideas. This word connects the ideas and that's why it matters." These students' thoughtful replies thrilled me; I was very excited that they considered the importance of this transitional word in so much careful and metacognitive detail.

> **New Literacy Connection**
>
> A contemporary and relevant way to help students grasp the importance of the transitional language is to have them view scenes from movies or television shows they enjoy, and narrate the events using transitional language. This helps them see how important and widely used transitional language is, and how difficult it would be to tell a story without it. I like to ask students to do this at home on their own so that they will use television shows or movies in which they are especially interested. When they come in the next day, I ask students to share their narrations and to identify the transitional language they used. Upon completing this activity, one student exclaimed to me, "Wow! We use these transition words all the time!"

3. Ask students to identify transitional language in published writing and analyze its significance.

Once you're comfortable with your students' understandings of the importance of this writing strategy, I suggest giving them more ownership by asking them to identify transitional language in published writing, and then to analyze its significance to the original passage. This activity, which students can do in small groups or individually, calls for students to find a passage from a published text that contains transitional language, rewrite the passage without that language, and then reflect on why the transitional language is important to the original passage. This activity is similar in some ways to the previous step, but differs in the amount of responsibility placed on the students. Instead of the teacher finding a published example of transitional language, showing it and a revised example to the students, and then leading a discussion on the differences, students conduct their own identification, revision, and analysis.

When conducting this activity with your students, I recommend giving each individual or group (depending on how you've chosen to structure the task) the chart depicted in Table A5 (Appendix A), and asking them to look through their own books, as well as those available in the classroom, to find passages with transitional language. After the students take some time to find and analyze their examples, I like to circulate the room and confer with them. In this chapter's classroom snapshot, I described a conversation I had with a student group that found and analyzed a passage from *Escape from Mr. Lemoncello's Library.* This group did an excellent job finding a passage that uses the transitional word "but" and reflecting on its significance.

Another group with which I worked during that lesson chose the following passage from Bruce Coville's book *My Teacher Flunked the Planet*: "As the end of the mission drew closer, the dreams got worse. Also Susan and I noticed something strange . . ." (Coville, 1992: p. 95). After a student in the group shared this passage with me, another read the revised version, which was altered to no longer include the transition word "also": "As the end of the mission drew closer, the dreams got worse. Susan and I noticed something strange . . ." Finally, the group shared its thoughts on the importance of this transitional language; "Without 'also,'" explained one student, "this would sound strange. It wouldn't fit together like it does." When I asked the student to elaborate on the idea of the elements of the passage "fitting together," she stated, "This word makes everything [in the passage] make sense. One thing happened, and another thing also happened. Without the word 'also,' it's harder to make sense of what's going on. It just sounds like a list." This student's comparison between a clearly structured passage that uses transitional language effectively and a disjointed list of events showed me that she had developed a strong understanding of this concept.

4. Have students apply the writing strategy of using transitional language to their own narratives.

Now that students have studied, revised, and analyzed transitional language in published texts, it's time to move to the next step of this instructional process, in which students apply this writing strategy to their own narratives. I give my students the following directions to follow when putting this writing tool into action:

♦ Review your narrative for any places where you've used transitional language. Check to see that the transitional words and phrases you've used make sense and logically connect the information you're telling the reader.
♦ Review your narrative for any places where you transition between ideas but don't use transitional language. If there are,

68 ♦ Narrative Writing Strategies

> add transitional language that enhances the clarity and flow of your narrative.
>
> ♦ As you continue to write, be aware of events and ideas in your narrative that would be as clear as possible if connected by transitional language. Include the transitional language that best fits these situations.

While the students work on using transitional language in their own narratives, I recommend conferring with them individually. In these conferences, I ask the students to show me the transitional language they've used in their work, and explain why they used the specific transitional words and phrases they did. This gives me insight into the students' understanding of this strategy and helps me clear up any confusion they have. I also look over their narratives to see if there are any sections that would be further enhanced with the addition of transitional language.

I recently conferred with a student who was working on a narrative about Paul Revere's Ride for his social studies class; this student explained that he used "a lot of transitional words" in his narrative, highlighting specifically the following excerpt as an example (see Figure 5.2).

After showing me this example, the student pointed out that he used the transitional phrase "for example" in the second sentence and the transitional word "however" in the third. In the next instructional recommendation, we'll examine why this student felt the transitional language he used was important to the quality of his narrative.

5. Help students reflect on the importance of transitional language to their own works.

Figure 5.2 Student Narrative Containing Transitional Language

Paul Revere made a lot of journeys for Boston's Committee of Safety. For example, he frequently went to places like New York and Philadelphia. However, his most famous journey was just around the Boston area, where he lived. On April 18th, 1775, he rode all around the Boston area in order to tell other people that the British troops were coming.

I recommend completing this instructional process by asking students to reflect on the importance of transitional language to their own narratives. To help students engage in this reflection, I present them with the following questions: (1) "Why is transitional language important to the effectiveness of your narrative?" and (2) "How would your narrative be different if you didn't use transitional language?" The student who used the transitional terms "for example" and "however" in the previously described piece about Paul Revere asserted that these examples of transitional language enhance his narrative: "The transitional words, 'for example' and 'however,' that I used make my writing make a lot more sense. They connect things I'm saying about Paul Revere to other things. 'For example' shows that I'm giving an example, and 'however' shows that his most famous journey was different from his others." He continued to explain, "My narrative about Paul Revere would be different if I didn't use transitional words because it just wouldn't make as much sense. I wouldn't be able to say that things are similar or are different, so it would be harder for people reading to figure out what I'm saying."

Final Thoughts on Including Transitional Language

- The writing strategy of including transitional language in narrative writing is addressed in Common Core State Writing Standards W.3.3.C, W.4.3.C, W.5.3.C, W.6.3.C, W.7.3.C, and W.8.3.C.
- "Transitional language" consists of words and phrases that establish a connection or relationship between events and ideas.
- It's important to note that transitional language doesn't just link ideas and events that are similar; writers also use transitional language when the ideas in statements differ.
- Transitional language is important to strong narrative writing because it increases the sense of flow in a piece of writing and communicates clearly how two events and ideas relate to each other.
- Without this writing tool, a narrative would feel disjointed and would not directly convey to readers how aspects of the piece are similar or different.
- When teaching students about including transitional language:
  - show students examples of published texts that incorporate transitional language;
  - discuss with students why transitional language is an important concept to effective narrative writing;
  - ask students to identify transitional language in published writing and analyze its significance;

- have students apply the writing strategy of using transitional language to their own narratives;
- help students reflect on the importance of transitional language for their own works.

6

Using Concrete Words and Phrases

What Does "Using Concrete Words and Phrases" Mean?

Strong narrative writers do not use vague, general terms that are hard to understand. Instead, they incorporate specific, concrete words and phrases that clearly communicate their intended meanings to readers. The Common Core State Writing Standards address the significance of this writing tool, as Standards W.4.3.D, W.5.3.D, W.6.3.D, W.7.3.D, and W.8.3.D identify the use of concrete words and phrases as important to effective narrative writing. In this chapter, we'll explore the following: what "using concrete words and phrases" means; why this strategy is important to strong narrative writing; an example of a lesson on this concept; and instructional recommendations for helping your students use concrete words and phrases in their own narrative writings. In addition, we'll examine published mentor texts that use concrete words and phrases especially well and discuss what makes those examples effective.

Let's begin by considering what it means to use concrete words and phrases in narrative writing. To make their works as clear and understandable as possible, writers frequently use concrete words and phrases known as specific nouns and strong verbs. We'll consider each of these concepts individually.

Specific Nouns

Specific nouns are those that clearly identify a particular entity (such as a person, place, thing, or idea). A narrative writer who uses this concept will avoid general terminology such as "boat" or "car" and will, instead, use much more specific terms such as "kayak" or "jalopy" in their place. Specific nouns are classified as concrete words and phrases because of the

♦ 71

72 ♦ Narrative Writing Strategies

Table 6.1 Specific vs. General Nouns

Specific Nouns	General Versions
couch	furniture
mall	building
football	sport
saxophone	musical instrument

Table 6.2 Strong vs. Weak Verbs

Strong Verbs	Weak Verbs
hurled	threw
devoured	ate
screamed	said
gazed	looked

precise ways they convey certain images to readers. Table 6.1 lists some specific nouns and corresponding general nouns that the specific versions could replace.

Strong Verbs

Strong verbs describe actions in concrete, easy-to-understand ways. When you read a piece of writing that contains strong verbs, you will have no doubt how the characters' actions were performed. For example, a writer focusing on strong verb use would not describe their afternoon walk by saying they "went" around the neighborhood, as this nonspecific (or "weak") verb could be interpreted in a number of ways. Instead, they would use a strong, specific verb like "strolled" or "wandered" that creates clear images in a reader's mind. Table 6.2 depicts some strong verbs alongside weaker versions of them.

Why Using Concrete Words and Phrases Is Important to Effective Narrative Writing

Concrete words and phrases are important tools for effective narrative writing. The use of specific nouns and strong verbs ensures that a piece's readers visualize the same imagery that the author originally intended, avoiding any possible confusion. For example, let's say that an author wanted to show that a character moved through a room in a sneaky, discreet way.

This author would be best served using a strong verb such as "crept" to ensure readers understand this action and envision it clearly. If the author had otherwise used a weak verb like "moved" instead of "crept," readers wouldn't know how the character moved; this weak verb would make it unlikely that readers would envision this action as the author originally intended.

Now, let's take a look at how published authors use this writing strategy and consider its importance to their works. In her novel *The Sisterhood of the Traveling Pants*, Ann Brashares (2001) utilizes strong verbs and specific nouns to help readers clearly envision the situations she describes. The sentence "Sweat dripped down from her thick, dark hair onto her neck and temples" (p. 107) employs both tactics; "neck and temples" are specific nouns that illustrate exactly where the character's sweat fell, and "dripped" is a strong verb that reveals the particular way it happened. If we replaced this concrete language with more general versions, we could create the sentence "Sweat *fell* down from her thick, dark hair onto her *body*." While this version still expresses basic information, it doesn't provide the concrete imagery that Brashares' original work does. Instead, the revised sentence limits the reader's understanding of the situation; it doesn't tell us how or where the sweat fell, while the concrete language in the original text provides this information.

The writing tool of concrete words and phrases also has a major impact on Jerry Spinelli's *Maniac Magee* (1990). In the sentence "George McNab pulled himself up from the easy chair and shuffled back into the kitchen" (p. 163), Spinelli uses the strong verb "shuffled," and the specific noun "easy chair" to vividly depict an event for his readers. Without this concrete language, Spinelli's narration would be much more vague, as readers might encounter a sentence such as "George McNab pulled himself up from the *furniture* and *walked* back into the kitchen." This revised passage replaces the strong verb in the original passage with the weaker version "walked," and swaps the original specific noun with the more general word "furniture." When I read the revised sentence, I have a hard time visualizing this event; I wonder what kind of furniture George McNab was using and the exact way he walked into the kitchen. However, Spinelli's original passage creates a specific image in my mind; I can clearly picture where McNab was sitting, and the specific manner in which he went to the kitchen.

As these excerpts from Brashares' and Spinelli's works reveal, the use of concrete words and phrases is an important component of strong narrative writing. Without the use of specific nouns and strong verbs, readers may not envision the events in these passages as the authors originally intended. While general nouns and weak verbs have multiple possible meanings, the concrete versions of these concepts do not; instead, they contribute to the effectiveness of narratives by providing readers with specific understandings of events, ideas, and images. In the next section, we'll look

74 ♦ Narrative Writing Strategies

inside a seventh-grade classroom, and examine how the students in that class explore the clarity provided by this writing tool.

A Classroom Snapshot

"That was probably the most interesting homework assignment I've ever done," a seventh grader tells me at the beginning of class.

"Glad to hear it!" I reply. "I'm excited to see how all of you did with it."

In our last class meeting, I gave the students a homework assignment that called for them to apply their knowledge of concrete words and phrases to programs they watched on television. To complete this task, the students needed to:

♦ watch a televised show, movie, or event;
♦ write a brief description of something that happened in the show, movie, or event, using a specific noun and strong verb in the narration;
♦ rewrite that description, replacing the specific noun and strong verb in the sentence with more general versions;
♦ write a brief reflection of how the two sentences are different.

"Let's get started," I tell the class, "Who wants to tell us what he or she did for the assignment?"

"Ooh, I'll start," responds a young lady in the front of the room. "I had fun with this, too! I watched a rerun of the show *iCarly*. My description of what happened, the one that uses strong verbs and specific nouns, is 'Spencer dashed into the iCarly Studio.'"

"Great," I reply. "Now, can you tell us what strong verbs and specific nouns you used that sentence?"

"Definitely," answers the student. "I used the strong verb 'dashed' to show how Spencer entered the room, and I used the specific noun 'iCarly Studio' to show the room he entered."

"Really nice," I say, praising the student's work. "How would that sentence read if you replaced that specific noun and that strong verb with more general versions?"

"I wrote," the student responds, "that it would be 'Spencer went into the room.'"

"And how do you feel that sentence is different from the original one that uses specific language?"

"It's doesn't really tell you much. The first sentence that I made, it tells you a lot, like the exact way Spencer went into the room and exactly what room he entered. The second sentence that I made, it doesn't tell that exact information. You know he went into a room, but you don't know the details that the first sentence tells you."

Using Concrete Words and Phrases ◆ 75

"Wonderful job!" I reply. "I love the way you identified all of the specific information that the original passage tells readers, and how you explained that the revised sentence with general language does not."

Several other students share their responses; one explains that he watched a basketball game and created the sentence "LeBron James heaves up a three-pointer," which he then turned into the more general "LeBron James throws up a shot." He then compares the sentences by describing how readers can clearly picture what's taking place in the original sentence, while the revised text can be interpreted in a number of ways. After a number of volunteers have shared, I proceed to connect last night's homework with today's in-class activity.

"Today," I inform the students, "we're going to build on the work you did for homework last night by working on an activity that's similar in some ways to your homework assignment, but different in others. You'll work in groups, and each group is going perform several related tasks: find a published sentence that uses a specific noun and strong verb; identify the specific noun and strong verb in the sentence; replace those words with more general versions; and reflect on the differences. Before you get started, I want for us to take a look at an example together."

I place the graphic organizer depicted in Table 6.3 on the document camera (a blank, reproducible version of this graphic organizer is available in Appendix A).

Table 6.3 Model of Concrete Language Analysis

Published Sentence that Uses Concrete Language	Concrete Language in Sentence	Revised Version with General Language Instead of Concrete Language	Your Analysis of the Difference in the Sentences
"I've got guts," Jerry murmured, getting up by degrees, careful not to displace any of his bones or sinews. (Cormier, 1974: p. 7)	Strong verb: Murmured Specific nouns: Bones or sinews	"I've got guts," Jerry *said*, getting up by degrees, careful not to displace any of his *body parts*.	The second version still gives you a basic description, but doesn't provide nearly as much specific information. The strong verb "murmured" tells you exactly how Jerry said what he did and the specific noun phrase "bones or sinews" lets you know the exact body parts to which the narration is referring.

76 ♦ Narrative Writing Strategies

"As you can see," I tell the students, "I selected a sentence from *The Chocolate War* [Cormier, 1974] that uses a specific noun and strong verb, identified those concepts in the sentence, replaced them with general examples, and wrote an analysis of how the two sentences are different." I read the information on the chart out loud as the students follow along. Afterwards, I explain that in their small groups the students will be doing the same kind of work on this activity: "I'm going to give each group a blank version of this handout. Once you have the handout, look through the books in the classroom, as well as your own books, for a sentence that contains a specific noun and a strong verb. Once you find that sentence, write it down and then keep going by filling out the rest of the information on your chart."

I distribute a handout to each group and watch as the students scour the books in the classroom for examples of concrete language. After the students take some time to find their examples and start discussing them, I begin to circulate and check in with the student groups. I first speak with a group working with the book *Theodore Boone: The Abduction*, a young-adult novel by John Grisham (2011).

"Hey everyone," I say, sitting down with the group. "Did you find concrete language in your book?"

"Yes, we did," responds a student. "We picked out a sentence we like that has a specific noun and a strong verb here on page 107: 'In the hall, he whipped out his cell phone and called Ike.'"

"Awesome job finding that sentence," I reply. "Tell me what specific noun and strong verb you identified here."

Another student in the group answers: "For the specific noun, we picked out 'hall' because it tells you where in the school building Theo [the book's protagonist] was. For the strong verb, we picked out 'whipped' because that word shows the exact way he took out his phone."

"That's wonderfully said," I praise the student. "I love how you shared your reasoning regarding why you selected each word as a concrete language example. The next column on your chart asks you to rewrite the sentence with general instead of concrete language. What did you come up with for that?"

"We changed it to," responds a student, "'In the building, he took out his cell phone and called Ike.' We changed 'hall' to 'building' and we changed 'whipped' to 'took.'"

"Fantastic!" I reply. "Now for the final task: the reflection section, which asks you to analyze the differences between the two sentences. How did you feel the original sentence and the revised version were different?"

"They're different," answers a group member, "because of how much more specific the first one is. That one says specifically where he was—in the hall—and specifically how he took out his phone—he whipped it out. The revised version doesn't say those things specifically."

"Excellent!" I tell the student. "You all did a wonderful job on every component of this activity—you selected a sentence with concrete language, identified concrete language in it, revised the sentence to contain more general language, and reflected on the importance of the concrete language in the original text. Awesome work!"

Recommendations for Teaching Students About Using Concrete Words and Phrases

In this section, I describe a step-by-step instructional process for teaching students about the writing strategy of using concrete words and phrases—specific nouns and strong verbs—in narrative writing. The instructional steps I recommend are:

1. Show students published examples of specific nouns and strong verbs.
2. Talk with students about why specific nouns and strong verbs are important to effective writing.
3. Work with students as they analyze the significance of specific nouns and strong verbs to published texts.
4. Have students apply the strategy of using concrete language to their own narratives.
5. Ask students to reflect on why the specific nouns and strong verbs they used are important to the success of their narratives.

Each of these recommendations is discussed in detail in this section.

1. Show students published examples of specific nouns and strong verbs.

I recommend introducing the writing tool of using concrete words and phrases to students by showing them published texts that contain specific nouns and strong verbs. This helps them formulate strong understandings of what these concepts look like and how writers use them. When I introduce this writing strategy to my students, I provide brief explanations of specific nouns and strong verbs to build their background knowledge, and show them the examples in Tables 6.1 and 6.2, to help them to understand the differences between these examples of concrete language and more general versions of them. Next, I show them excerpts from published texts that contain these concepts; for example, I recently showed my seventh graders the following sentence from Peg Kehret's (2004) novel *Abduction!*: "Matt stared out the car window, fighting nausea" (p. 62).

After displaying this sentence on the document camera and reading it aloud to the students, I identified "stared" as a strong verb in the sentence and "nausea" as a specific noun, and discussed why they fit those criteria. I explained that "stared" is a strong verb because it allows readers to picture exactly how this action was performed, and "nausea" is a specific noun for a similar reason, as it enables readers to understand exactly what Matt was fighting. Seeing this writing concept used in published works increases its authenticity; while explaining the concepts of specific nouns and strong verbs without making connections to published texts can result in abstract lessons that students have difficulty grasping, showing students published examples of these concepts in action illustrates that professional writers use concrete language to make their works as strong as possible.

2. Talk with students about why specific nouns and strong verbs are important to effective writing.

I recommend continuing this instructional process by helping students understand why the specific nouns and strong verbs you identified in the previous step are integral to strong narrative writing. To do this, I suggest showing students the published sentence containing concrete language that you shared with them in the first step of this process, as well as a revised version of this sentence with the strong verb and specific noun replaced with more general language. For example, after showing my seventh graders the sentence "Matt stared out the car window, fighting nausea," described in the previous recommendation, I showed them a new version without the strong verb and specific noun I discussed with them: "Matt looked out the car window, fighting illness."

Once you show students these versions, talk with them about the significance of the concrete language. For example, after I showed my students both versions of the sentence about Matt, I led a discussion on why the specific noun and strong verb in the original passage are important to its success. When talking with my seventh graders about these sentences, I asked them to compare the effectiveness of the verbs "stared" and "looked," to which one student replied, "No question, 'stared' is so much better. It's because of how specific it is. When I say 'stared,' you know exactly what kind of action I'm talking about. When I say 'looked,' well, that could be done a whole bunch of ways." Another student shared a similar comparison of "nausea" and "illness," saying "I think the word 'nausea' is a good word to use here because 'illness' can mean a lot of things. 'Illness' is way more general." These students' explanations revealed their understandings of the importance of the concrete language used in this sentence to the story's effectiveness.

3. Work with students as they analyze the significance of specific nouns and strong verbs to published texts.

Once you're comfortable with students' understanding of the importance of concrete language for effective writing, I suggest asking them to look through published texts, identify specific nouns and strong verbs in those texts, and analyze the importance of those terms. I've found that this activity can increase student engagement, while also giving them more responsibility for their learning, as it calls for them to select examples from books of their choosing, and apply the skills of identification and analysis they've learned in the first two steps of this instructional process to those selections. A seventh grader recently explained to me that he enjoyed the opportunity for choice in this activity: "It was cool to be able to look for [concrete language] in the books we like. That made it more interesting for me. I love *Holes*, so it was cool to find examples in that book."

When conducting this activity, which can be done individually or in small groups, give the students blank versions of the handout depicted in Table 6.3 (available in reproducible form in Table A6, Appendix A) and then meet with them as they select and analyze specific nouns and strong verbs in their independent reading books or texts they choose from the classroom library. In this chapter's classroom snapshot, I described my conversation with a group that used the book *Theodore Boone: The Abduction* by John Grisham. Another group with which I spoke during the same class period did similarly strong work with a sentence from Lemony Snicket's (2013) novel *When Did You See Her Last?* The group selected the sentence "I slipped the needle out of the tire" (p. 55), identifying "slipped" as a strong verb and "needle" as a specific noun. Next, the students in this group revised the sentence to read, "I moved the object out of the tire," replacing "slipped" with "moved," and "needle" with "object." Once the group shared this information with me, I inquired into their analysis of the differences between the sentences; one student explained that the concrete language in the original text is important because of how much it enables him as a reader to visualize the event: "When I read the first sentence, I can picture that; I can see in my mind what it looked like. The concrete language lets you do that. When I read the second sentence, I can't really see it in my mind. Concrete language really makes a difference."

4. Have students apply the strategy of using concrete language to their own narratives.

I recommend continuing this instructional process by giving students even more ownership and responsibility over their work with concrete language. In this fourth step, the students work on their own narratives and focus on applying the writing tools of specific nouns and strong verbs to their works. When preparing my students to do this, I ask that they first look over what they've written up to that point, identify any weak verbs or general nouns, and replace those words or phrases with more concrete language. I then tell the students that, after they've done this, they should keep writing their narratives, focusing on using specific nouns and strong verbs while doing so.

Figure 6.1 Student Work Example of Concrete Language

> Oh no! This natural phenomenon only happens every 18 months, but I detest it when it does! The moon's orbit has totally intersected with mine, which has blotted out my light and blanketed everyone below in darkness. This is called a total solar eclipse and it happens when the moon gets between the Earth and me, the sun.

I recently worked with a student who applied the writing strategy of using concrete language to a narrative description of total solar eclipses. In this narrative, an excerpt of which is depicted in Figure 6.1, he used strong verbs and specific nouns to explain the procedure of a solar eclipse from the point of view of the sun.

This student uses the specific nouns "natural phenomenon" and "orbit" to help readers clearly understand the concepts in his narrative. These specific terms are especially important since the student wrote this piece to not only tell an engaging story, but also to reveal his understanding of the scientific concept of total solar eclipses. Similarly, the strong verbs in this piece—such as "blotted out" and "blanketed"—effectively depict the actions in the passage, ensuring the reader envisions what the writer intended, while also showing the author's awareness of the events that take place during a total solar eclipse.

New Literacy Connection

Many of the students I work with love to create videos on technological devices (such as the school's tablets), so I created a way to connect this interest in making video recordings with the narrative-writing strategy of using concrete words and phrases. I ask the students to work in groups to create sentences with specific nouns and strong verbs, and then to act out these sentences, recording videos of them doing so on the tablets. I then ask the same student groups to revise those sentences to include general nouns and weak verbs and then act out those versions, again recording videos of them doing so. Creating video recordings of these sentence versions not only engages students, but also helps them see how sentences with concrete language are much clearer and easier to interpret than those with vague words and phrases.

5. Ask students to reflect on why the specific nouns and strong verbs they used are important to the success of their narratives.

This final step focuses on students' metacognitive awareness of the importance of concrete language to the narratives they're creating. I recommend helping students reflect on the significance of this writing tool to their works by asking them two related questions: (1) "Why is the use of strong verbs and specific nouns important to the success of your narrative?" and (2) "How would your narrative be different if you didn't use the strong verbs and specific nouns that you did?" I posed these questions to the student who created the previously described narrative about total solar eclipses. He explained that "strong verbs and specific nouns are really important [to the success of his narrative] because of how clear they make everything." He continued to identify particular examples of concrete language in his piece and comment on their significance: "When I use the strong verb 'blanketed,' well, that makes things clear because it shows what the darkness is like for people on earth. And when I say 'natural phenomenon,' I use a specific noun that makes it clear that total solar eclipses are part of nature." This student reflected on how his narrative would be different if he didn't use strong verbs and specific nouns: "The narrative just wouldn't make as much sense without them. If I said 'thing' instead of 'natural phenomenon,' it wouldn't make as much sense because people wouldn't understand what's happening as much. Same for 'blanketed'; if I said it 'put' people in darkness, it would be harder to understand because 'blanketed' shows you what's happening more clearly."

Final Thoughts on Using Concrete Words and Phrases

- Using concrete words and phrases in narrative writing is addressed in Common Core State Writing Standards W.4.3.D, W.5.3.D, W.6.3.D, W.7.3.D, and W.8.3.D.
- To make their works as clear and understandable as possible, writers frequently use concrete words and phrases known as specific nouns and strong verbs.
  - Specific nouns are those that clearly identify a particular entity (such as a person, place, thing, or idea), such as the more specific "kayak" instead of the more general "boat."
  - Strong verbs describe actions in concrete, easy-to-understand ways, such as the verb "strolled" instead of the vaguer verb "went."
- Concrete words and phrases are important tools for effective narrative writing because the use of specific nouns and strong verbs ensures that readers of a piece are visualizing the same imagery that the author originally intended, avoiding any possible confusion.

82 ◆ Narrative Writing Strategies

- ◆ When teaching students about using concrete words and phrases:
  - ◆ show students published examples of specific nouns and strong verbs;
  - ◆ talk with students about why specific nouns and strong verbs are important to effective writing;
  - ◆ work with students as they analyze the significance of specific nouns and strong verbs to published texts;
  - ◆ have students apply the strategy of using concrete language to their own narratives;
  - ◆ ask students to reflect on why the specific nouns and strong verbs they used are important to the success of their narratives.

7

Creating Sensory Details

What Does "Creating Sensory Details" Mean?

Have you ever read a narrative and pictured yourself in the middle of the story, seeing, hearing, touching, smelling, and tasting the same things as the characters? Narrative writers create these experiences for their readers by using sensory details, a concept identified as important by Common Core State Writing Standards W.4.3.D, W.5.3.D, W.6.3.D, W.7.3.D, and W.8.3.D. In this chapter, we'll examine: what "creating sensory details" means; why this writing tool is important to strong narrative writing; a description of a lesson on this concept; and specific suggestions for helping your students create sensory details in their own narratives. In addition, we'll look at ways published authors include sensory details in their works and discuss what makes those examples especially effective.

So, what exactly *is* this narrative-writing tool? The term "sensory details" refers to information in a piece of writing that allows readers to understand how they would use their senses to experience events and situations in the text, enabling readers to know what the characters in narratives can see, smell, taste, touch, or hear. Let's explore this concept further by taking a look at the following passage from Jim Arnosky's *The Pirates of Crocodile Swamp:*

> Jack set up our tiny stove on the beach and heated our frying pan full of salt water to cook the crabs he had caught earlier. When the water was boiling, I plopped in the crabs. After a few minutes, their blue shells turned bright red, and we had fresh crabmeat for lunch. Being cooked in salt water made the meat extra salty, but we didn't mind. It tasted good to us.
>
> (Arnosky, 2009: p. 92)

84 ◆ Narrative Writing Strategies

Table 7.1 Sensory Details in an Excerpt from *The Pirates of Crocodile Swamp*

Sense	Sensory Details from Text
Sight	'their blue shells turned bright red'
Sound	'I plopped in the crabs'
Taste	'Being cooked in salt water made the meat extra salty'

In this passage, Arnosky uses a number of sensory details, which help readers clearly understand the characters' experiences cooking and eating crabs on the beach: "their blue shells turned bright red" appeals to the sense of sight; "I plopped in the crabs" conveys a sound; and "Being cooked in salt water made the meat extra salty" connects to the sense of taste. Table 7.1 depicts the excerpts identified above, and the senses with which they're aligned.

Why Creating Sensory Details Is Important to Effective Narrative Writing

The writing strategy of creating sensory details is important for effective narrative writing for two related reasons: it provides readers with clear descriptions of characters' experiences; and enables writers to focus on particular aspects of situations. First, let's consider the idea that, without sensory details, it would be much more difficult for readers to envision the scenarios authors describe, as these details convey specific and concrete information about key aspects of narratives. To illustrate this, we'll examine Table 7.2, which juxtaposes the passage from *The Pirates of Crocodile Swamp* we've been discussing with what it might look like without any sensory details.

Table 7.2 Passage from *The Pirates of Crocodile Swamp* with and without Sensory Details

Original Passage from *The Pirates of Crocodile Swamp*	Revised Version without Sensory Details
Jack set up our tiny stove on the beach and heated our frying pan full of salt water to cook the crabs he had caught earlier. When the water was boiling, I plopped in the crabs. After a few minutes, their blue shells turned bright red, and we had fresh crabmeat for lunch. Being cooked in salt water made the meat extra salty, but we didn't mind. It tasted good to us. (Arnosky, 2009: p. 92)	Jack set up the stove to cook the crabs he caught earlier. I put the crabs in the water at the appropriate time. When the crabs were ready, we ate them and liked them.

Comparing these two passages reveals how much information the sensory details in the original text provide: removing much of the sensory language from the original passage creates a new version that is not nearly as specific and engaging. Without it, readers still know the bare minimum of information about this event, but lose all of the language that allows them to form a detailed understanding of what's taking place.

The second reason that sensory details are important to effective narrative writing is that they allow writers to focus selectively on particular aspects of situations. When an author uses sensory language, they highlight details that are especially important to the event or image being described. For example, in the previously described passage from *The Pirates of Crocodile Swamp*, author Jim Arnosky focuses on the senses of sight, sound, and taste in this passage, because those are the most important senses to the characters' experiences in this situation. At other points in the book, he invokes different senses that are particularly relevant to the events described there. In the following excerpt from his book, Arnosky uses details that connect primarily to the senses of smell and touch, which were not featured prominently in the passage we examined earlier:

> "Ugh!" he said. "Sandy, hold my nose. This stinks!"
> I held Jack's nose and my own. Jack chopped off the fish's head and peeled off its scaly skin.
>
> (Arnosky, 2009: p. 93)

The senses of smell and touch are highly relevant to this situation, as they align with the events Arnosky describes—Jack cutting off the head of an unpleasant-smelling fish and then peeling its skin.

When I speak with students about using sensory details in their works, I emphasize the purposeful use of this concept, explaining that it is a great way to add specific information about a piece of writing, but that it is also most effective when the author uses it to focus on images and details that are especially relevant to a situation. "If I'm writing about playing in a basketball game," I recently told a group of middle schoolers, "I should highlight sensory details that are related to playing in the game. For example, I don't feel my sense of smell has much to do with playing basketball, so I won't focus on that sense. Instead, I'll probably focus on sight, sound, and touch because those are the senses that I see as most connected to that particular situation. I'll describe seeing my teammates, hearing the crowd, and feeling the ball in my hands." After this discussion, I felt my students had a strong understanding of the importance of creating sensory details for effective narrative writing; this writing tool's ability to add specific details and to focus the reader's attention on particularly significant images. In the next section, we'll take a look inside an eighth-grade classroom, and examine how my students work to analyze the importance of this writing tool.

A Classroom Snapshot

"Today you're going to do something that might seem strange," I inform my eighth graders. "You're going to take a piece of writing and make it worse!"

The students look quizzically at me and I continue, smiling: "Don't worry, I'll explain. You've been doing a great job in previous classes on the narrative-writing strategy of creating sensory details. Remember how, in our last class, we talked about the importance of this writing strategy and looked at published passages that contain sensory details alongside revised versions with the sensory details removed?"

Many of the students in the class nod; some respond in the affirmative. "Well," I tell them, "today we're going to take that activity to the next level. We're going to split up into groups and I'm going to ask each group to find a published example of sensory details from the classroom library or your independent reading books, rewrite that example, eliminating as much of the sensory detail as you can, and then write a reflection on why the sensory details are important to the original example. As you can see, like I said earlier, you're taking a piece of writing and making it worse by removing the sensory details, but you're doing more than that: you're also analyzing the importance of this writing tool to the original passage."

I explain to the students that, before they work in small groups on this activity, I'm going to show them an example. I place the chart depicted in Table 7.3 and explain the information on it to the students, identifying the sentence from Gary Paulsen's (1985) book *Dogsong* I selected, sharing the new version I revised to eliminate sensory details, and describing my analysis of the significance of these details to the original passage.

After I describe the information on this chart to my students, I ask them what they think about the differences between and the importance

Table 7.3 Example of Sensory Detail Analysis

Original Passage	Revised Version with Sensory Details Omitted	Why the Sensory Details Are Important to the Original Passage
The frozen seal meat started to melt and give off oil immediately and the caribou began to cook in the oil and soon the smell of the meat filled the room and he liked that. (Paulsen, 1985: p. 8)	The frozen seal meat started to melt and give off oil immediately and the caribou began to cook in the oil.	The sensory details in the original passage highlight the smell of meat that the characters are cooking. Without these details, we don't have as clear of an understanding of what the characters are experiencing. With the details, we have a much more developed understanding of the situation.

of the sensory details. One student replies, "The first sentence sounds so much better. The sensory details make it much more descriptive and poetic-sounding."

"I agree," interjects another student. "It's like the sentence still makes sense without those details, but it doesn't sound nearly as good."

"Well said, both of you," I respond. "The sentence without sensory details is not nearly as descriptive and doesn't give us the full context of the situation Paulsen describes. This is the same kind of work you're going to do in your small groups. We're going to get into groups and I'll give each group a handout containing the same chart I just showed you, but you'll fill this one out with your own findings and ideas."

I divide the students into groups and give them copies of the chart to use for the activity (see Table A7, Appendix A, for a reproducible version of this chart). Impressed by how quickly they get started, I praise their efforts: "I love how you all got started so quickly on this activity. Each group looks so focused! After a few more minutes, I'll start meeting with each group. I'm looking forward to hearing your thoughts!"

After the students have taken some more time to work, I sit down with my first group: four students who are working with the book *Million Dollar Throw* by Mike Lupica (2009).

"Hey everyone," I greet the students. "I was really impressed by how engaged you all looked during this activity." The students smile and I continue: "Tell me what you found. What did you pick out from this book as an example of sensory detail?"

"There was a lot of sensory detail in it," answers a student in the group, "but we actually liked the first sentence in the book the best of all." He reads the book's first sentence aloud:

> This was always the best of it for Nate Brodie, when he felt the slap of the ball in his hands and began to back away from the center, when he felt as if he could see the whole field, and football made perfect sense to him.
>
> (Lupica, 2009: p. 1)

"I can definitely see why you picked that sentence!" I respond. "So well written! Before we move on, talk to me about the sensory details you noticed."

Another student in the group replies: "We noticed sensory details when the author says 'felt the slap of the ball in his hands' and when he says 'see the whole field.' The first of those has to do with the sense of touch and the other with sight."

"Nice job," I praise the student. "I love how you identified the statements that you felt contained sensory details and also noted the sense to which each one relates. Now, let's talk about how you changed this sentence. How did you revise it to omit sensory details?"

"We turned it into this: 'This was always the best of it for Nate Brodie, when he had the ball in his hands and began to back away from the center and football made perfect sense to him,'" answers a student. "We took out the sensory details about feeling the slap of the ball and about seeing the field."

"Very good," I tell her. "I love how you not only omitted those sensory details, but also identified the specific sensory details you omitted. That definitely shows your awareness of this concept. The final step is to reflect on the importance of the sensory details to the original passage. What do you all think—why is this writing tool important to Mike Lupica's original sentence?"

"It's really important," explains a student, "because it really explains the situation. Without the details of feeling the slap of the ball and seeing the field, we don't really know why Nate liked what he was doing so much."

"I thought the sensory imagery helped me think I could put myself in the situation," adds another student. "It helped me feel the slap of the ball and see the field too. Without it, I couldn't."

"Wonderful job!" I exclaim. "I love how you two commented on how the sensory detail in the original sentence gives us information about why Nate enjoyed what he was doing so much and how it helps us put ourselves in the same situation. Your comments really show your understanding of the importance of this concept in general, and to this sentence in particular. Awesome work!"

Recommendations for Teaching Students About Creating Sensory Details

In this section, I describe a step-by-step instructional process for teaching students about creating sensory details in narrative writing. The instructional steps I recommend are:

1. Show students published examples of sensory details.
2. Discuss with students why sensory details are important to effective narrative writing.
3. Have students identify sensory details in published texts and analyze their significance.
4. Ask students to incorporate sensory details in their own narrative writing.
5. Help students reflect on the importance of sensory details to their works.

Each of these recommendations is described in detail in this section.

1. Show students published examples of sensory details.

This initial step enables students to see how the writing strategy of creating sensory details looks in practice, providing them with concrete understandings of how writers apply this tool to their works. I recommend showing students a published excerpt that contains multiple sensory details and working together with them to identify those details. For example, I recently showed a group of middle schoolers an example from Wilson Hawthorne's novel *The Last Pirate* during our initial conversations about sensory details:

> I kept looking over the charts until, after a while, it started to rain. Nothing put me to sleep quicker than the sound of rain hitting the metal roof of our mobile home. My eyes got tired first. I looked over at Hammerhead. He was already snoring. I put everything away on top of the dresser and turned off the light. My room wasn't dark, though. The streetlight outside the window takes care of that. I could read by it if I wanted to.
>
> (Hawthorne, 2009: p. 55)

I placed this passage on the document camera and read it aloud with the students following along. Afterwards, the students and I discussed the sensory details Hawthorne uses, noting that the details in this paragraph relate to the senses of sound and sight. I recommend identifying at least one sensory detail for your students and then asking them what other ones they notice. This gradually releases responsibility onto them and engages them more than if you identify all of the examples for them. After I pointed out the sensory detail of "the sound of rain hitting the metal roof" and connected it to the sense of sound, I asked the students what sensory language they noticed. One quickly pointed out that the sound of Hammerhead (the narrator's dog) snoring is another sensory detail, while another noted that "the details about the streetlight have to do with sight." Once you've shown students one published passage containing sensory details, I recommend showing them another excerpt from either the same book, or from a different one that includes details related to some other senses and leading a similar discussion. This lets students see how writers include different kinds of sensory details in their work, accentuating the versatility of this writing tool.

2. Discuss with students why sensory details are important to effective narrative writing.

After showing students published examples of sensory details, I recommend talking with them about why this concept is important to strong narrative writing. Doing so helps students begin to think metacognitively about why one might apply this writing strategy to their work. I like to

90 ♦ Narrative Writing Strategies

begin these discussions by juxtaposing published examples that contain sensory details (such as the ones I discussed in the first recommendation) with revised versions of these examples that no longer contain the same sensory details. For example, I recently showed my students the information in Table 7.4, which places the previously described excerpt from *The Last Pirate* alongside a new version, which has been changed to omit key sensory details.

Once we read these passages, my students and I discussed what sensory details present in the original text did not appear in the revised version, as well as why those original details are important to the effectiveness of Hawthorne's original passage. I pointed out that the sensory details in the second sentence related to the sound of the rain were no longer present in the revised passage, and a student commented that the details about Hammerhead snoring were also omitted. Another student volunteered that the original passage contained details related to the sense of sight in its final two sentences, which comment on the presence of light in the room, while the revised text does not.

Following the identification of these omitted details, I led a discussion on the importance of this writing tool to this passage, and to narrative writing in general. I explained to the students that the use of sensory details provides clear descriptions of what's taking place in a story, and allows writers to focus on certain aspects in depth. Using the passage from *The Last Pirate* to illustrate my points, I told the students, "The sensory details in this section of *The Last Pirate* really give us a strong description of what's going on; we can imagine the sound of the rain, of the dog snoring, of the light from outside. If Hawthorne didn't use these details, we couldn't imagine this scene as clearly."

I then asked the students why they thought Hawthorne used details related to the senses of sound and sight: "Why did he choose details related to these senses and not others?"

Table 7.4 Passage from *The Last Pirate* with and without Sensory Details

Original Passage from *The Last Pirate*	Revised Version without Sensory Details
I kept looking over the charts until, after a while, it started to rain. Nothing put me to sleep quicker than the sound of rain hitting the metal roof of our mobile home. My eyes got tired first. I looked over at Hammerhead. He was already snoring. I put everything away on top of the dresser and turned off the light. My room wasn't dark, though. The streetlight outside the window takes care of that. I could read by it if I wanted to. (Hawthorne, 2009: p. 55)	I kept looking over the charts until, after a while, it started to rain. I felt sleepy. My eyes got tired first. I looked over at Hammerhead. He was asleep. I put everything away on top of the dresser and turned off the light.

"Because," answered a student, "those are the most important ones to what's happening here."

"That's right," I responded. "Authors use sensory details especially effectively when they pick ones that most relate to the events of a particular scene. That's another way they can make writing stronger. Hawthorne focuses on details related to this scene with his sensory descriptions, and that really makes this passage effective."

3. Have students identify sensory details in published texts and analyze their significance.

The third step of this instructional process is even more interactive than the previous two, as it calls for students to work in small groups or individually to find passages in published texts that contain sensory details, revise them in a way that omits key sensory details, and analyze the importance of the sensory details to the original passage. When conducting this activity with your students, I recommend first modeling an example for them, as I describe doing in this chapter's classroom snapshot. When modeling this example, use Table A7, in Appendix A, and fill it out by selecting and analyzing a published sentence of your choice. Talk with the students about the sentence you've chosen, how it looks without key sensory details, and why those sensory details are important. I recommend involving the students in the conversation about the significance of these details; this helps engage them and gives you a chance to evaluate their understandings of this writing tool.

When you think the students are ready, give them copies of Table A7 and ask them to get started by selecting a published passage containing sensory details that they will use to complete the activity. I like to allow the students several minutes to identify a passage and begin analyzing it before I circulate the room and confer with the individuals or groups. I recently met with a student group that completed this activity using an excerpt from the book *Moon over Manifest* by Clare Vanderpool (2010). They selected the sentence "Smoothing out the yellowed newspaper for the thousandth time, I scanned the page, hoping to find some bit of news or insight into my daddy" (p. 2). One of the students in the group commented astutely on the presence of sensory details in the sentence, saying, "The first part of this sentence has a lot of sensory details—'smoothing' tells about the feeling, or the sense of touch, and 'yellowed' tells about how it looks, or the sense of sight." The group revised its sentence to omit these sentence details, creating "I scanned the page, hoping to find some bit of news or insight into my daddy." After sharing this revised version with me, a group member explained her belief about the importance of sensory details to the original text: "The sensory details are important because they let you totally picture what's happening. I can totally picture what's happening in the [original] sentence, but I can't picture what's happening in the second one. In the revised one we made, you can't imagine [the narrator] smoothing the page or seeing the yellow paper."

New Literacy Connection

Students' interests in online content can provide a great opportunity for them to practice creating sensory details. As a homework assignment or in-school follow-up activity, students can find images online and describe them using relevant sensory details. I recently assigned this activity for homework with my eighth graders and was thrilled with what they found; one student selected a picture of a county fair and crafted a wonderful description that incorporated details related to sounds, sights, smells, and tastes. Afterwards, he commented on how much he enjoyed the activity: "This was really fun. I love fairs, so I loved finding a great picture of a county fair online and describing it. Plus, the sensory details helped me describe it."

4. Ask students to incorporate sensory details in their own narrative writing.

After your students have completed the first three steps of this instructional process, I recommend giving them more ownership of their learning by asking them to apply the writing strategy of creating sensory details to their own narratives. Before I ask the students to do this, I talk with them about the best ways to incorporate sensory details into narrative writing. I explain that narrative writers use sensory details most effectively when incorporating them in descriptions of important features of the story's setting and of key events. Discussing this information with the students helps them understand the most strategic ways to use this strategy.

When it's time for the students to get started, I tell them to first look over their narratives for any descriptions of settings or events that could be improved with the addition of sensory details, and add sensory details that would enhance these descriptions. Once they've done that, I explain that they should continue writing their narratives, looking for ways to incorporate sensory details in setting and event descriptions while they write. As the students work, I meet with them individually to check on their progress. In these meetings, I ask students to identify examples of sensory details in their writing and explain what senses they incorporated in these descriptions. This lets me evaluate the students' understanding of this concept and how effectively they're using it in their works. I recently conferred with a student who was writing a narrative set at the beach. In our conversation, she explained that she revised her original text to include sensory details about the sights, smells, and sounds at the beach to help readers imagine the scene: "I put in a lot of sensory details to describe what Julie [the protagonist and narrator] saw, smelled, and heard when she first got to the beach on vacation. I didn't have these at first—I went back and put them in. I think this part of the story's a whole lot more descriptive now."

5. Help students reflect on the importance of sensory details to their works.

I recommend concluding this instructional process by asking students to think metacognitively and reflectively about the importance of sensory details on their own narrative writing. To facilitate this in-depth thinking, I like to ask students two reflection questions: (1) "Why is the use of sensory details important to the narrative you're writing?" and (2) "How would your narrative be different without the sensory details you included?" While these questions specifically ask students to comment on the use of this writing tool in the narratives they're currently creating, they also promote thinking about the significance of this strategy in general. The student who wrote the narrative about the beach, described in the last recommendation, commented on the importance of sensory details to her work: "I think [sensory details] make a huge difference in my story! They make things come to life much more. I think the ones I used let you put yourself right at the beach with Julie." She continued to explain how she feels her narrative would be different without its sensory details: "The story would be so much more basic. It wouldn't come to life like it does. I don't think readers would enjoy the story as much because they couldn't put themselves right next to the characters like they can now."

Final Thoughts on Creating Sensory Details

- ♦ Creating sensory details in narrative writing is addressed in Common Core State Writing Standards W.4.3.D, W.5.3.D, W.6.3.D, W.7.3.D, and W.8.3.D.
- ♦ The term "sensory details" refers to information in a piece of writing that allows readers to understand how they would use their senses to experience events and situations in the text, enabling readers to know what the characters in narratives can see, smell, taste, touch, or hear.
- ♦ The writing strategy of creating sensory details is important to effective narrative writing for two related reasons:
  - ♦ It provides readers with clear descriptions of characters' experiences.
  - ♦ It enables writers to focus on particular aspects of situations.
- ♦ When teaching students about creating sensory imagery:
  - ♦ show students published examples of sensory details;

- discuss with students why sensory details are important for effective narrative writing;
- have students identify sensory details in published texts and analyze their significance;
- ask students to incorporate sensory details in their own narrative writing;
- help students reflect on the importance of sensory details to their works.

8

Crafting a Strong Conclusion

What Does "Crafting a Strong Conclusion" Mean?

Recently, I spoke with an eighth grader who was having an unexpected problem with a narrative he was writing: he didn't know how to end it. "I can't think of a good way to conclude the story. I don't want to just stop the action, but I don't want to write a summary either. This is harder than I thought it would be!" While I was unhappy to hear about this student's troubles, I was heartened by how seriously he was taking the writing tool of crafting a strong conclusion. The Common Core State Writing Standards also acknowledge the importance of this aspect of narrative writing, as Standards W.3.3.E, W.4.3.E, W.5.3.E, W.6.3.E, W.7.3.E, and W.8.3.E call for students to craft effective conclusions to their narratives. In this chapter, we'll explore the following: what "crafting a strong conclusion" in narrative writing means; why this concept is important to the effectiveness of a narrative; a description of a lesson on this concept; and key recommendations for helping your students craft strong conclusions to their own narratives. While delving into these concepts, we'll look at conclusions from published narratives and consider what makes those conclusions effective.

Let's begin by examining what it means to craft a strong conclusion in narrative writing. A conclusion is a final section of a narrative that provides a sense of closure to the story's events and leaves readers with a final message related to those events. Table 8.1 describes each of these conclusion components.

In the book *The Last Pirate*, author Wilson Hawthorne crafts a conclusion that provides a sense of closure and leaves readers with a final

♦ 95

96 ♦ Narrative Writing Strategies

Table 8.1 Conclusion Components

Component	Description
Sense of closure	The sense of closure in a conclusion comes from wrapping up the narrative's events; it is often achieved by resolving the story's conflict and describing the fate of the piece's main characters.
Final message	The final message in a conclusion is an insight or idea with which the author leaves readers; it often relates to the theme of a story, or a lesson a character learned during the narrative's events.

message. In the book's final passages, Hawthorne reveals that Harley, the book's narrator from a financially struggling family, has received a new boat and a great deal of money that he can use to support his mother. In addition, Hawthorne explains that Harley has established a romance with Eden, a girl for whom he had repeatedly expressed his interest throughout the book. The book closes with a conversation between Harley and Eden, and with Harley's comments to the reader:

> She slugged me in the arm. "You don't even have a watch," she laughed.
> "Well, neither do you."
> "Know what else you don't have?"
> "What's that?"
> "A first mate," she said.
> "You looking for a job?"
> "More like a partnership."
> "Seal it with a kiss?"
> The tide carried us out to sea.
> Life is a roller coaster, right? Hang on and enjoy the ride. And write some history you'd let anybody read. That's my advice.
> At that moment, I was hanging on with both arms and all my heart. And out on the sea next to his island, I finally understood what turned that old pirate around.
> Some diddie, huh?
>
> (Hawthorne, 2009: p. 213)

Harley's new boat and relationship with Eden provide a sense of closure by resolving the book's financial and romantic storylines, and his statements at the end of the book leave readers with a final message by providing his insights about life, which he has gained from the experiences described in the book. In the next section of this chapter, we'll take this discussion a step further by exploring why conclusions like this one are important to effective narrative writing.

Why Crafting a Strong Conclusion Is Important to Effective Narrative Writing

A strong conclusion is an especially important component of an effective narrative because the information it provides is essential to the reader's understanding and enjoyment of a text. Without the closure and final message provided by a strong conclusion, a narrative would feel incomplete and confusing; readers might wonder if the story is actually over and what the big ideas in the narrative are.

Let's illustrate the importance of a strong conclusion by examining the last paragraph of Jerry Spinelli's novel *Maniac Magee*. Protagonist Maniac Magee is homeless for most of the novel; early in the book, he comes to a racially divided town called Two Mills, where he makes friends with both Caucasian and African-American children, helping resolve the town's racial tensions. Maniac, who is Caucasian, is eventually adopted by the African-American Beale family and develops a strong friendship with their daughter Amanda, who is mentioned in this passage:

> Maniac said nothing. He was quite content to let Amanda do the talking, for he knew that behind her grumbling was all that he had ever wanted. He knew that finally, truly, at long last, someone was calling him home.
>
> (Spinelli, 1990: p. 184)

This passage provides readers with closure to the book's events, showing what Maniac's life is like with his new family, and with reduced racial tensions in Two Mills. In addition, it leaves readers with a final message, emphasizing the importance of being part of a family, and feeling the sense of security that accompanies having a family and a home. This conclusion is representative of the importance of this writing tool to the narrative in which it is found. If Jerry Spinelli did not conclude *Maniac Magee* in this way, the novel would produce a less satisfying experience: it wouldn't tie the novel's events together in such a clear, meaningful way or clearly convey its message.

When I discuss the importance of crafting effective conclusions with my students, I explain that a strong conclusion is important because it leaves readers with two related thoughts: "We want our readers to finish reading the conclusions to our narratives and think 'That author wrapped up the events of that story really nicely, with a good sense of closure,' and 'That author left me with a clear final thought about the story's events.' We don't want our readers to finish reading our narratives and think 'I can't

98 ♦ Narrative Writing Strategies

actually tell if the story is over or not,' and 'I don't know what the author wants me to get out of that book.' A narrative with a strong conclusion won't leave its readers asking those questions."

A Classroom Snapshot

"Today, we're going to examine a book you've already read as a class this year," I tell my eighth graders, "but we're going to do it in a totally different way."

"What book?" inquires a student.

"*Seedfolks*," I reply, referring to the narrative by Paul Fleischman (1997) that the students read at the beginning of the school year.

"Oh, I really like that book!" the student exclaims.

"Great," I continue, smiling. "In our class today, we're going to connect *Seedfolks* with the narrative-writing strategy of crafting a strong conclusion that we've been discussing this week."

Today is my third day discussing strong conclusions with these students. In our first session on this topic, the students and I discussed what it means to create a strong conclusion in narrative writing. We talked about the conclusion components described in Table 8.1, and explored how the previous concluding text from *The Last Pirate* embodies those components. In our second meeting about this writing tool, we considered why crafting strong conclusions is important to effective argument writing, focusing on ways well-crafted conclusions, like the one from *Maniac Magee*, discussed in this chapter, enhance the reader's enjoyment and understanding of a text. In today's class, I'm going to put more ownership on the students by asking them to work in groups to identify conclusions to specific narratives in *Seedfolks* (the book is divided into a series of related stories told from different characters' points of view), point out how the conclusion in their group's passage meets the criteria of a strong conclusion, and explain why this conclusion is important to the effectiveness of the story in which it is found.

I describe these directions to the students and then explain that we'll work on an example together before I ask them to do so in small groups: "Let's start by taking a look at an example of what I'll ask you to do when you work on this activity. Does anyone remember the name of character who tells the first story in *Seedfolks*?"

"It's Kim!" answers a student.

"That's right," I respond. "Since Kim tells the first story, we'll get started by taking a look at how I analyzed the conclusion to her section. Then, once we all understand what to do, you'll work in groups, with each group taking on a different story from the book."

I place the chart depicted in Table 8.2 on the document camera and talk through its components with the students, explaining how the final paragraph of Kim's story provides readers with a sense of closure and a final message, and then discussing why this concluding section is important to Kim's narrative.

Next, I tell the students that it's their turn to work on a version of this activity. I divide the students up into small groups, assign each group a specific character from *Seedfolks*, give each student a copy of the book from the school's resource room, and provide each group with a blank version of the template depicted in Table 8.2 (see Table A8, in Appendix A).

"This is a great opportunity for you to show the knowledge you've developed about strong conclusions in our classes this week," I encourage the students. "And, you get to do it using a book you've already read this year and that I hear a lot of you really liked. Use the chart to guide you and think about all of its components. After you identify and write down the concluding text, talk with your group members about the next three components—how it provides a sense of closure, how it provides a final message, and why it's important to effectiveness of its narrative. This activity is asking you to really analyze how a conclusion does what it does and why it's important. It's not easy to analyze writing in this way, but I know you all can do it!"

Giving the students some time to get started on their analysis, I watch and listen as they identify the conclusions to their sections and analyze their components and effectiveness. Once it seems like the groups have made significant progress, I begin to check in with them about their work.

Table 8.2 Conclusion Analysis

Conclusion	How it Provides a Sense of Closure	How it Provides a Final Message	Why it Is Important to the Effectiveness of the Narrative
My class had sprouted lima beans in paper cups the year before. I now placed a bean in each of the holes. I covered them up, pressing the soil down firmly with my fingertips. I opened my thermos and watered them all. And I vowed to myself that those beans would thrive. (Fleischman, 1997: p. 4)	This passage provides a sense of closure to Kim's narrative by showing that she has completed her quest to plant lima beans in honor of her deceased father. She wanted to do this to honor him and has succeeded in doing so.	This conclusion provides readers with the final messages of determination and family. Kim was determined to plant these beans in a vacant lot and succeeded in doing so; she did so to honor her father in a way that was meaningful to her.	This passage is important to the effectiveness of its narrative because of the way it concludes Kim's quest to plant lima beans, and emphasizes the significance of this action.

100 ◆ Narrative Writing Strategies

I first meet with a group working with the *Seedfolks* narrative told from the point of view of Gonzalo, an eighth grader from Guatemala. This narrative describes Gonzalo's experience interacting with his great-uncle, Tio Juan, who recently immigrated to the United States. Since Tio Juan has a difficult time adjusting to life in his new country, Gonzalo compares him to a helpless baby. However, Gonzalo's opinion of Tio Juan changes toward the end of the story when Tio Juan starts working in a garden, a place where he feels comfortable. In the book's concluding paragraph, Gonzalo describes watching Tio Juan plant seeds and discusses how that experience causes him to view his great-uncle differently.

I begin my conversation with the student group focusing on this narrative by praising their efforts: "You all worked so thoroughly on this activity. You wrote down so many thoughts and ideas and you were all so involved in your group conversations!"

"Thanks," a group member says, smiling. "We all said this was one of our favorite stories from *Seedfolks*."

"Awesome," I reply. "Let's get started. What did you identify as the conclusion of Gonzalo's story?"

"This part right here," answers a student. "I'll read it."

He proceeds to read the final paragraph of the story, in which Gonzalo explains his changing perception of Tio Juan:

> He showed me exactly how far apart the rows should be and how deep. He couldn't read the words on the seed packet, but he knew from the pictures what seeds were inside. He poured them into his hand and smiled. He seemed to recognize them, like old friends. Watching him carefully sprinkling them into the troughs he made, I realized that I didn't know anything about growing food and that he knew everything. I stared at his busy fingers, then his eyes. They were focused, not far-away or confused. He changed from a baby back into a man.
>
> (Fleischman, 1997: p. 22)

"Great job sharing that," I tell the student. "Now," I address the whole group, "I'm really excited to hear your analysis of this conclusion. The next column on the chart asks for your thoughts on how this conclusion provides a sense of closure. What do you think about that?"

"I think it gives a good sense of closure," replies a student in the group, "because of how it talks about Tio Juan turning back into a man. It's like he turned back into his original adult self when he was gardening."

"That's really nicely said," I reply. "There's a sense of coming full-circle in this conclusion: Tio Juan was an adult in Guatemala, then he was like a child in a way when he first came to America, and now he seems more like an adult to Gonzalo. Next, the chart asks for your thoughts on how the conclusion provides a final message to readers. What kind of final message did you notice?"

"We thought there were really two final messages," answers another student. "One was that you should respect your elders, because Gonzalo learns to respect Tio Juan in the end. Another final message was that it's important to do what you love, because once Tio Juan does what he loves—planting seeds—he doesn't seem like a baby anymore."

"Fantastic!" I exclaim. "I love how you identified both of those messages. Your final comment about the importance of doing what you love is especially insightful. Tio Juan no longer seems out of place once he's planting the seeds. Once he does so, he's comfortable and well-adjusted. Let's focus now on the final column, which asks why the conclusion is important to the effectiveness of the narrative."

"I think it's totally important," responds a group member, "because of how it completes the whole way Tio Juan turned back into a man, into his old self. He was starting to do that in the parts [of the narrative] right before the conclusion, but the conclusion paragraph really completes it and totally shows him as a man."

"Also," states another student in the group, "it's important because of the final messages it gives. Those final messages—you should respect your elders and it's important to do what love—are really emphasized in the conclusion."

"Both of your comments are spot-on," I reply. "The conclusion definitely reveals the completion of Tio Juan's transformation and it provides important emphasis on the narrative's final messages. Wonderful work, you all."

Recommendations for Teaching Students About Crafting a Strong Conclusion

In this section, I describe a step-by-step instructional process to use when teaching students about crafting a strong conclusion in narrative writing. The instructional steps I recommend are:

1. Show students examples of strong conclusions from published narratives.
2. Talk with students about why crafting a strong conclusion is an important component of effective narrative writing.
3. Ask students to analyze the conclusions to published narratives.
4. Confer with students as they craft conclusions in their own narrative writing.
5. Have students reflect on why strong conclusions are important to their own narratives.

102 ♦ Narrative Writing Strategies

I discuss each of these recommendations in detail in this section.

1. Show students examples of strong conclusions from published narratives.

I recommend beginning this instructional process by showing your students published examples of strong conclusions, and then using those examples to introduce the major components of conclusions: a sense of closure and a final message. For example, when introducing the narrative-writing strategy of crafting strong conclusions to the eighth-grade class described in this chapter, I showed them the previously featured conclusion from the novel *The Last Pirate,* and pointed out how author Wilson Hawthorne uses the concluding text of that book to provide the novel with a sense of closure, and leave readers with a final message related to the book's events.

I've found that using a published example to introduce these attributes of conclusions to students makes the features much more accessible than they would be if I explained the ideas of providing a sense of closure and delivering a final message without connecting those ideas to published works. If I simply told my students about these conclusion components without providing any specific examples, it may be much harder for them to understand these ideas. In contrast, showing students concrete examples gives them specific touchstone texts where they can examine and see the features of effective conclusions in action. When showing your students examples of conclusions, I recommend discussing texts with which they are familiar if possible, as this can increase their comfort with the piece and their ability to look at the conclusion for its major components instead of figuring out the plot first. However, if there is a published conclusion from a work that the students haven't read, and that you believe to be an especially good example of a conclusion's components, you can use that, also. Just be sure to give the students the background information they need about the story's plot and characters so that they can focus on the aspects of the conclusion instead of the basic events of the narrative.

2. Talk with students about why crafting a strong conclusion is an important component of effective narrative writing.

Once you've shown your students published examples of strong conclusions and identified the key components of those conclusions, I recommend building on this conversation by talking with students about the importance of these conclusion attributes for effective narrative writing. This discussion takes the previous one a step further, as it goes beyond identifying the components of strong conclusions to discussing their importance. When leading this conversation with your students, I suggest showing them a published conclusion (I prefer to use a different conclusion from what I showed them in the first step to provide a variety of examples), work with them to identify how the conclusion provides a sense of closure and delivers a final message, and then discuss with them why it is important to the narrative that the conclusion performs these functions.

The final component of this step—considering the importance of the conclusion's sense of closure and final message—helps students think metacognitively about the importance of a strong conclusion to an effective narrative. When I discuss these ideas with students, I help them consider what the narrative as a whole would be like if the conclusion did not contain these components. To do so, I point out text that represents each of these conclusion aspects, and explain why each aspect is important to the overall story. For example, I'll identify language that provides readers with a sense of closure to the piece, and talk with students about why it's important that a narrative has a sense of closure, and what readers' experiences would be like if it didn't. Next, I'll point out how the conclusion provides readers with a final message about the narrative's events and characters, and discuss with them the impact that this message can have on readers. While the specific ideas I'll share vary, based on the information and ideas in different conclusions, some of the points I make remain consistent: the sense of closure in a narrative is important because it communicates clearly to readers how the piece's events have been resolved, and the final message is important because it identifies major ideas and themes that the author wants readers to take from the piece.

3.   Ask students to analyze the conclusions to published narratives.

Next, I recommend continuing this instructional process by asking students to identify and analyze the conclusions of published narratives. This activity, an example of which is described in this chapter's classroom snapshot, gives students increased responsibility for their learning by asking them to complete four related steps: (1) identify the conclusion to a published narrative; (2) analyze how the conclusion provides a sense of closure to its narrative; (3) analyze how it delivers a final message related to the narrative; and (4) comment on why this conclusion is important to the effectiveness of the narrative.

I recommend asking students to use texts they've already read for this activity, as familiarity with the story's events will help them dive into their analyses without needing to decipher the plot. In the activity discussed in the classroom snapshot, I used the book *Seedfolks* that the students had previously read. Since this book is divided into narratives told from different characters' points of view, I modeled an example using one of these narratives, and then asked students to work in small groups, with each group analyzing the conclusion of a different narrative in the book. Although the use of this book was effective, this activity can also work well with other text types. Students can all analyze the conclusion to a book they've read together, each student can analyze the conclusion to their independent reading book, or student groups that have read in-common books as part of a literacy circle can analyze the conclusion of the text their group read. No matter which of these ways you choose to organize the activity, be sure to give each student or group a copy of the template in Appendix A (Table A8), give them some time to get started, and then confer with them, asking them to share their thoughts and analyses.

I've found that the increased student ownership associated with this activity can enhance student engagement, while also providing me with an opportunity to gauge my students' understanding of this concept more closely. If students' analyses suggest that they are struggling to identify and analyze aspects of conclusions, I take additional time to reteach whatever information the students need. Once I'm comfortable with all of the students' understandings, I move to the next part of this process, in which students craft effective conclusions to their own narratives.

4. Confer with students as they craft conclusions in their own narrative writing.

This step gives even more ownership and responsibility to the students, as it calls for them to apply what they've learned about creating strong conclusions to their own narrative writing. However, this aspect of the instructional process still calls for teachers to play active roles by conferring with the students. When I recently introduced this activity to my students, I told them, "It's time for you to put the writing tool of crafting strong conclusions into action in your own narrative writing. While you work on writing your narratives, I'm going to confer with each of you. In these conferences, I'm going to ask you to identify your piece's conclusion, and explain how the conclusion provides readers with a sense of closure and a final message." Focusing the conferences on these key conclusion components shows me whether the students understand these concepts well enough to incorporate them into their own writing. If a student's comments suggest that they don't understand the concepts very well, I use the conference to reteach any problematic topics.

> **New Literacy Connection**
>
> Students can connect new literacies and strong conclusions by including images in a narrative's conclusion that represent the final message the conclusion conveys to the reader. For example, the student writing the previously described narrative about a Pittsburgh Steelers quarterback who reconnects with his brother incorporated an image of a uniformed football

player walking out of a stadium with his family after a game. According to this student, this image captured the final message of family and togetherness he wanted readers to take from his narrative: "The big idea of this story is Sam coming together with his brother Jeff. Togetherness and family are really important ideas to this story and this picture shows those." Including this image helped this student to reflect on important issues in his narrative, while also working in the multimodal way that new literacies provide.

5. Have students reflect on why strong conclusions are important to their own narratives.

The final step of this instructional process, asking students to reflect on why strong conclusions are important to the effectiveness of the narratives they've written, helps students think metacognitively about the significance of this writing tool. To guide students' reflections, I recommend asking them two related questions about the importance of their conclusions: (1) "How does your conclusion enhance readers' experiences reading your narrative?" and (2) "How would your narrative be different without your conclusion?" These questions encourage the students to think about the positive impact that effective conclusions have on narratives, and help them consider what the work would be lacking without this concept.

I recently spoke with a middle schooler who had just finished reflecting on the conclusion to a narrative he had created about a boy who discovered he could predict the future. In this student's narrative, Jordan, the book's protagonist, uses his predicting powers to save another student with whom he did not previously get along. The student author explained that his conclusion enhanced his narrative by emphasizing its message of helping others and putting aside differences: "My conclusion made my narrative better because it talks about the story's message of not holding a grudge and giving a hand to people who need help." He continued to say that, without his conclusion, his story wouldn't emphasize that message as much: "If I didn't have a conclusion, I wouldn't have talked about that message as much as I did. Without the part when I talk about the message, the story just isn't as good."

Final Thoughts on Crafting a Strong Conclusion

- ♦ Crafting a strong conclusion in narrative writing is addressed in Common Core State Writing Standards W.3.3.E, W.4.3.E, W.5.3.E, W.6.3.E, W.7.3.E, and W.8.3.E.

- A conclusion is a final section of a narrative that provides a sense of closure to the story's events, and leaves readers with a final message related to those events.
- The sense of closure in a conclusion comes from wrapping up the narrative's events; it is often achieved by resolving the story's conflict and describing the fate of the piece's main characters.
- The final message in a conclusion is an insight or idea with which the author leaves readers; it often relates to the theme of a story, or to a lesson a character learned during the narrative's events.
- A strong conclusion is an especially important component of an effective narrative because the information it provides is essential to the reader's understanding and enjoyment of a text.
- Without the closure and final message provided by a strong conclusion, a narrative would feel incomplete and confusing; readers might wonder if the story is actually over and what the big ideas in the narrative are.
- When teaching students about crafting a strong conclusion:
  - show students examples of strong conclusions from published narratives;
  - talk with students about why crafting a strong conclusion is an important component of effective narrative writing;
  - ask students to analyze the conclusions to published narratives;
  - confer with students as they craft conclusions in their own narrative writing;
  - have students reflect on why strong conclusions are important to their own narratives.

Section 2

Putting It Together

9

Assessment Strategies

How Should We Assess Narrative Writing?

Throughout this book, we have explored a wide range of writing tools that enable elementary and middle-school students to create effective narratives. However, a key question remains: "How should teachers assess these narrative-writing tools?" I recommend evaluating students' narratives in a way that mirrors the toolkit approach to instruction: by separately evaluating students' use of each of the key components of narrative writing. I suggest doing this by using distinct rubrics that represent the particular standards of quality for each aspect of effective narrative writing.

I recently spoke with a group of teachers who shared that their students learned better when being evaluating on individual narrative-writing attributes. One explained that the concrete feedback made writing easier for her students to understand: "I have students who will say, 'Oh, I'm a bad writer,' but they're really not. What happens is they struggle with one writing trait and get bad overall feedback, and then they say they're bad writers. They really just need to improve their writing in certain areas. Evaluating this way shows them that." Another teacher shared a similar insight, stating that her students comprehended feedback better when it was divided into distinct narrative-writing components: "This makes it easier for them to understand what I'm saying about their writing because it becomes easier for them to see what they're doing well on and what they're not yet doing well on."

A number of these teachers also commented that evaluating students' narratives, using distinct rubrics for particular writing strategies, improved their experiences providing feedback. "I find giving feedback

♦ 109

110 ♦ Putting It Together

this way to be much better than just giving students an overall grade and comment," asserted one teacher. She continued to say, "Doing it this way is easier for me to understand, because giving the individual scores for different writing elements helps me keep track of how the students are doing." Another teacher explained that assessing student writing in this way made it easier for her to justify her students' grades: "I sometimes have parents ask me to explain why their child earned a certain grade. Now that I use this system, where I have a specific grade for each element of the child's written work, it's so much easier to explain why they earned the grades they did." These teachers' comments indicate ways that this assessment approach can enhance the evaluation experience for both students and teachers. Let's now examine particular criteria you can use when assessing your students on their uses of each of the argument writing tools described in this book.

Engaging and Orienting the Reader

When I evaluate how well my students have engaged and oriented the readers of their narratives, I focus on two key assessment criteria: (1) if the piece's introductory text captures the reader's interest and encourages them to continue with the narrative; and (2) if this opening section begins to introduce key information about the narrative, such as who the main characters are, where the story takes place, and what is taking place. I tell my students that I will evaluate them on these criteria because they represent what an effective introduction to a piece of narrative writing should do. "I should read the introductory part of your narrative," I tell them, "and get a sense of each of these attributes. I should feel like the piece is trying to hook me, to get me interested, and I should feel like I'm getting a first look at important information about the characters, setting, and conflict."

You may recall the student work described in Chapter 1, in which the author introduces a narrative about a Pittsburgh Steelers player who grew up rooting for the team. I explained to this student that his piece scored highly on this writing trait "because it immediately grabs the reader's attention, and clearly introduces the narrative's main character, setting, and situation." Table A9 (Appendix A) lists the evaluation questions I use when assessing the effectiveness of students' introductions—please note that the rubric depicted in this table, like all of the rubrics in this chapter, contains both evaluation questions and a place for comments so that you can explain to your students how they've used the concept effectively and how they can further improve in the future. (Reproducible versions of all the rubrics in this chapter can be found in Tables A9–A16, in Appendix A.)

Organizing an Event Sequence

Another key element of strong narrative writing is the organization of the piece's event sequence; a narrative without a clear sequence of events would confuse and frustrate readers. When evaluating how well a narrative's event sequence is organized, I consider the following ideas: (1) if the piece contains all of the aspects of narrative sequence (exposition, rising action, climax, falling action, and resolution); (2) if the aspects of narrative sequence are presented in order; and (3) if the aspects of narrative sequence can be clearly determined. These criteria allow me to evaluate students on whether they incorporated the components of narrative sequence, and how effectively they did so. Table A10 (Appendix A) depicts the criteria I use to determine how well students have organized the event sequences in their narratives.

I recently evaluated a narrative written by a fifth grader that scored highly on this component of narrative writing because it contained all aspects of narrative sequence, presented them in order, and distinguished between the components by organizing them effectively and discussing in detail. I told him his ability to differentiate between these elements was especially impressive: "I was really struck by how well you distinguished between all of these aspects of narrative sequence. Your story is organized really well, and each component is described in detail—it's very clear which section is the exposition, which is the rising action, which one is the climax, which is the falling action, and which one is the resolution. Awesome job!"

Developing Experiences and Events

I evaluate how effectively my students have developed the experiences and events in their narratives by considering the following criteria: (1) if the narrative describes experiences and events in detail, using components such as the event's setting, a character's actions, a character's motivation, a conversation between characters, and a character's thoughts; (2) if the experiences and events described are significant to the narrative; and (3) if these descriptions communicate the importance of the experiences and events. These evaluation criteria are especially effective because they emphasize that students should provide detailed descriptions of their most important events in their narratives. I've worked with students who have described events in great detail, but still not used this strategy as effectively as they could have, because the experiences and events discussed in detail were not especially important to the narrative.

Another effective aspect of these criteria is how the first evaluation question provides a number of options for students to consider when applying this tool to their narratives. I suggest highlighting these various possibilities, as some options will be better suited to certain narratives than others. I recently read a student's narrative that discussed an important event by describing a character's actions and thoughts; I then read another, written by a different student, which used a detailed account of a conversation between two characters to discuss an

112 ♦ Putting It Together

important event in the narrative. The distinctions in how these students developed key events in their works illustrate various ways students can put this writing tool into practice. Table A11 (Appendix A) contains the rubric I use to assess how well students develop experiences and details in their narratives.

Incorporating Characterization

Incorporating characterization is a key component of effective narrative writing, as it provides readers with important information about the characters in the piece. When I assess my students on their uses of this writing, I focus on two related criteria: (1) if the narrative includes important information about characters that helps readers understand them; and (2) if the narrative conveys information about characters through behaviors such as actions, thoughts, and dialogue, and allows readers to infer those characteristics. These standards of quality allows me to assess both the presence of characterization in the narrative and the effectiveness of it, as they call for students to describe their characters through their behaviors instead of simply listing their attributes.

Think back to the student discussed in Chapter 4, who enhanced her narrative about a girl that loves horses by conveying this information through the protagonist's actions. After she revised her story to focus on showing her character's attributes instead of telling readers about them, her piece scored highly on its use of this writing tool. When I evaluated her work, I praised the specific ways she used her character's actions to reveal her interest in horses, as the characterization in her piece was much stronger with these concrete descriptions that enabled readers to make inferences about her protagonist's characteristics. Table A12 (Appendix A) depicts the evaluation criteria I use to assess students' uses of this strategy.

Including Transitional Language

When I evaluate how effectively my students include transitional language in their narratives, I focus on two key assessment criteria: (1) if the narrative contains transitional language that establishes relationships between events and ideas; and (2) if the transitional language communicates clearly and accurately how ideas and events relate to each other. These criteria allow me to assess whether or not my students use transitional language in their narratives, and how effectively they do so. I make a point of explaining to my students that it's not enough to just use transitional language in their narratives: "To score highly on using transitional language, you need to do more than just use this writing tool; you also need to use it in a way that clearly shows how the things you describe are related. For example, if you're linking two similar ideas, you'll want to use language like 'in addition' or 'also' that shows that things are similar. If you're connecting two ideas that are dissimilar, you'll want to say things like 'however,' or 'on the other hand,' to show these dissimilarities."

The student work sample described in Chapter 5 is a example of the effective use of this writing tool; the author uses transitional language such as "for example" and "however" to explain how the information in his narrative about Paul Revere's Ride. Without these transitional terms, his work would not be as effective and easy to understand. Table A13 (Appendix A) illustrates the evaluation criteria I use when assessing students on their uses of transitional language in their narratives.

Using Concrete Words and Phrases

The use of concrete words and phrases is another important tool for effective narrative writing. Concrete terms like specific nouns and strong verbs ensure that readers of a piece are visualizing the same imagery that the author originally intended, avoiding any possible confusion. I assess students' uses of concrete words and phrases by considering the following ideas: (1) if the narrative contains examples of concrete language, such as specific nouns and strong verbs; (2) if these examples of concrete language express specific information clearly; and (3) if the specific information expressed by the concrete language makes sense in the context of the narrative. I've found the third of these criteria to be especially significant, as it allows me to assess how well the students' use of concrete language aligns with the situation in which it is used. I explain this to my students by telling them that I want them to use concrete words and phrases, but I also want them to be sure that the words and phrases they're using work for their story: "We know that 'went' is a pretty weak verb and that there are a lot of stronger ones you could use instead, like 'sprint,' 'trudge,' or 'stroll.' But be sure that the strong verb you use is one that really fits in it with what you want to say."

Students who use concrete language that fits with the context of the narrative implement this strategy as effectively as possible. For example, the student work featured in Chapter 6 of this book contains concrete language that enhances the description of solar eclipses; the piece includes the strong verbs "blotted out" and "blanketed" that express specific information, and align with the actions that take place during these events. Other strong verbs may not fit with the topic of this narrative as well as these do. Table A14 (Appendix A) contains the evaluation questions I use when assess students on their uses of this writing tool.

Creating Sensory Details

Creating sensory details is important to strong narrative writing because of the ways these details convey how readers would use their senses to understand the piece; a narrative with strong sensory details communicates what the characters in the piece see, smell, taste, touch, or hear

114 ♦ Putting It Together

in particular situations. When I assess how well my students have used this writing tool, I focus on two evaluation criteria: (1) if the piece contains details that appeal to the reader's senses; and (2) if these sensory details highlight information that is especially important to the event or image being described. I explain to my students that the strongest narrative writers use sensory details that are especially relevant to particular situations; for example, if an author is describing a trip to a restaurant, they would focus on senses especially related to that experience, such as the smell of spices and taste of the food. If a particular sense isn't particularly related to an event, I explain that they should then omit imagery related to that sense and focus on those that are more relevant to the situation.

I recently worked with a middle schooler whose writing scored especially highly on this aspect. In his narrative about running a cross-country race, he used a number of sensory details when discussing the start of the race. He wrote about the sight of the runners' bright uniform colors, the feeling of being jostled by others at the crowded starting line, and the sound of the starting whistle. Not only did this writer use strong sensory details, but he focused on those that were especially relevant to this experience, keeping the reader focused on the most important components of his narrative. Table A15 (Appendix A) depicts the evaluation criteria I use when assessing students' uses of sensory details.

Crafting a Strong Conclusion

The final narrative-writing attribute I assess is the writing tool of crafting a strong conclusion. When I evaluate the quality of my students' conclusions, I focus on two key attributes: (1) if the conclusion provides readers with a sense of closure to the story's events; and (2) if it leaves readers with a final message related to those events. Each of these evaluation criteria aligns with an important feature of an effective conclusion: a conclusion with a strong sense of closure helps readers enjoy and understand the narrative, while one with an insightful final message emphasizes important themes and ideas in the work. I tell my students not to lose sight of the importance of a strong conclusion: "Sometimes writers assume that readers don't really need the information in the conclusion. In reality, good narrative writers know how important a conclusion is, and spend a lot of time making it as effective as possible."

I recently worked with a fourth grader who created a very effective conclusion to a narrative about bonding with her parents and siblings during a church retreat. In this conclusion, the author brought a sense of closure to the piece by explaining how she worked with her siblings and parents to complete a team-building activity. In addition, this author left readers with a final message about the closeness that developed between her and her family members, emphasizing this important idea. Without this sense of closure and final message, this narrative would not have been as effective: readers might ask whether or not it was actually finished and what the key ideas in the piece are. Table A16 (Appendix A) illustrates the evaluation criteria I use when assessing the effectiveness of students' conclusions.

A Note on Using These Evaluation Criteria

Whenever I discuss these evaluation criteria with teachers, I make sure to emphasize that it's not necessary to always assess students on all eight narrative-writing tools at once. Instead, I recommend beginning a unit on narrative writing by assessing students' works on two fundamental writing tools, such as engaging and orienting the reader, and organizing an event sequence. Once students have mastered these concepts, I suggest introducing new, more advanced writing strategies, such as using concrete words and phrases and creating sensory details, and evaluating students on those. Gradually increasing the amount and complexity of writing strategies on which we assess our students helps prevent them from feeling overwhelmed at the beginning of the evaluation process; a fifth-grade teacher recently shared with me that adding new evaluation criteria over time was effective with his students: "One reason I think my kids did a great job is that I didn't evaluate them on everything at once. I taught them some things to do when they write, evaluated them on those, and then taught them some more things and evaluated them on those."

Evaluating students on different writing tools also facilitates differentiation: some students might complete a narrative and be ready to be evaluated on all eight of the tools described in this book; others' needs might be best met by evaluating them on three or four of the most basic ones at that point in time, and then evaluating them on the other writing tools later in the school year when they've developed further as writers. I recommend taking advantage of the flexibility related to these writing tools to make your assessment as instructive for your students as possible.

Final Thoughts on Assessing Students' Narrative Writings

- ♦ I recommend separately evaluating each attribute of effective narrative writing in students' works by doing the following:
  - ♦ giving students rubrics that represent the standards of quality for specific writing tools;
  - ♦ providing separate scores and feedback for each student's performance on these distinct attributes.

116 ◆ Putting It Together

- Each of the writing tools discussed in this book represents an attribute on which students' narratives can be evaluated.
- Evaluating students on specific attributes provides clear feedback on which writing tools they have mastered and their remaining areas of need.
- You don't need to evaluate students on all eight narrative-writing tools at one time. I recommend beginning by assessing students' works on two fundamental concepts and then adding more complex ones over time.

10

Final Thoughts and Recommendations for Classroom Practice

How Can We Put the Ideas in This Book into Practice?

Think back to the opening paragraphs of this book's introductory chapter, in which I describe a workshop I conducted with elementary and middle school literacy teachers on narrative writing and the Common Core State Standards; in this description, I highlight my conversations with two teachers, Alexis and Julie, who have been teaching narrative writing for years, but were uncertain how to do so in the Common Core era. The narrative-writing tools and the corresponding toolkit approach described in this book can resolve the anxieties of teachers like Alexis and Julie, who are unsure of what aspects of narrative writing to focus on in their instruction, and the best instructional methods to use while doing so.

In this chapter, we'll examine seven key recommendations for putting the ideas in this book into practice:

1. Show students examples of specific narrative writing tools in published works.
2. Talk with students about why each one of these writing tools is important for effective narrative writing.
3. Engage students in activities in which they analyze the importance of specific narrative-writing tools.
4. Ask students to apply each of the narrative-writing tools to their own works.
5. Help students reflect on the importance of each of these writing tools on their narratives.
6. Facilitate connections to new literacies with your students.
7. Show students how narrative-writing tools are present in a range of content areas.

♦ 117

118 ◆ Putting It Together

The first five of these recommendations are instructional steps that help students understand the features of narrative writing, to think metacognitively about their importance, and then apply them to their own works. Recommendations six and seven describe ways to capitalize on the relevance and applicability of narrative writing, by making connections to new literacies and content areas that go beyond the boundaries of traditional language arts instruction. Let's explore these ideas in more detail!

Recommendation One: Show Students Examples of Specific Narrative Writing Tools in Published Works

Beginning this instructional process by showing students examples of specific narrative-writing tools in published works allows students to see what these writing tools look in practice, giving them concrete understandings of how published authors incorporate them into their narratives. If students only read general descriptions of writing strategies without examining specific published examples, they may not understand these strategies as clearly. When putting this recommendation into practice with your students, use this book's Annotated Bibliography, which identifies specific excerpts from published narratives, and connects each with a Common Core Writing Standard.

Once you've identified a narrative-writing excerpt you'd like to share with your students, be clear about the strategy you want them to examine. For example, if you want your students to take note of how a narrative uses sensory imagery, convey to students that this strategy is the lesson's focus, so that they'll know to concentrate on this feature as they read. Communicating this focus is especially important because many published passages can contain a number of effective writing strategies; for example, an excerpt that contains excellent sensory imagery can also engage and orient readers in the narrative. After students have examined published works with specific narrative tools in mind, they'll be ready to move to the next step of this process.

Recommendation Two: Talk with Students About Why Each One of the These Writing Tools Is Important to Effective Narrative Writing

This recommendation builds on the previous activity. Now that you've shown students examples of narrative-writing strategies in published texts, the next step is to discuss the importance of these writing tools for the texts in which they appear. These discussions help students think critically about the significance of these strategies for effective narrative writing, enabling them to think metacognitively about these concepts. I like to frame these conversations with my students by focusing on the purposeful nature of effective writing: "Authors do everything they do for specific reasons," I tell them. "All of the writing strategies we identify in published texts and then discuss are used by authors to make their works as effective as possible." I go on to explain that each writing tool is used with a specific goal in mind, connecting to the toolkit metaphor that is central to this book's approach.

When discussing the importance of a specific writing tool with your students, I recommend asking the students to consider what the narrative would be like if the author had not used that strategy. For example, if you are discussing the concept of using concrete words and phrases with your students, help them consider how the piece would be different if the concrete language in the piece was replaced with less specific alternatives. You can place the original text on a document camera and juxtapose it with a revised version, allowing students to compare the two and understand why the concrete words and phrases contribute to the effectiveness of the original work. This same tactic can be adapted for use with all of the writing strategies described in this book; comparing a text in which a writing tool is used with one in which it is not used can help students grasp its significance.

Recommendation Three: Engage Students in Activities in Which They Analyze the Importance of Specific Narrative Writing Tools

Once you have talked with your students about the importance of a particular writing strategy for effective narrative writing, I recommend asking them to work individually or in small groups on activities whereby they analyze the significance of that strategy in specific texts. These activities give students more responsibility for their learning by providing them with hands-on opportunities to apply the ideas they learned in the second recommendation to other examples of narrative writing. When constructing these activities, you'll want to create ways for your students to examine pieces of narrative writing and consider why a particular writing strategy is important to those examples.

So, how can these activities take shape in the classroom? Here is an example: when working on the writing tool of developing experiences and events, I ask students to select a detailed, descriptive passage from a book, write down that passage, turn it into a much more concise version that no longer contains detailed description, and finally, reflect on why the author chose to write a detailed, descriptive version of the passage instead of a brief, concise version. This series of activities gives students increased ownership of learning, as it asks them to select a passage that incorporates this strategy, revise it so it no longer contains the strategy, and analyze the strategy's importance to the text. While the specifics of these activities will vary somewhat as students focus on different strategies, the key elements of them should remain the same: students should look closely at examples of particular narrative-writing tools, work with them in a way that relates to the features of that concept, and analyze their importance to the narrative in which they appear.

Recommendation Four: Ask Students to Apply Each of the Narrative Writing Tools to Their Own Works

This instructional step continues to give students more ownership of and responsibility for their learning, asking students to apply their knowledge of specific writing tools to their own narratives. When I ask my students to use these strategies in their own narratives, I'll first ask them to examine what they've written up to that point and identify sections that can be improved by incorporating this strategy. Next, I'll instruct them to continue writing, keeping a lookout for instances when they can apply the strategy. For example, when preparing my students to apply the writing strategy of using transitional language, I'll ask them to evaluate the effectiveness of any examples of this concept they've already used, add transitional language to places in the text that can be improved by its inclusion, and then incorporate this strategy when appropriate as they continue to write. While my students write, I'll hold one-on-one conferences with them, in which I talk with the students about their use and understanding of the focal strategy. These meetings provide great opportunities to provide your students with individualized instruction related to the ways they're applying specific writing tools to their own works.

Recommendation Five: Help Students Reflect on the Importance of Each of These Writing Tools to Their Narratives

I believe that effective writing instruction includes a reflection component, in which students consider the importance of specific writing strategies for the works they've created. When I help my students reflect on the significance of a particular concept, I ask each of them to consider why that concept is important to the narrative they created, and how the piece would be different if they did not use it. Chapters 1–8 of this book each contain specific reflection questions aligned with those chapters' focal strategies. These reflection questions help students think metacognitively about the significance of the writing tools they're learning. Students who develop a metacognitive awareness of the importance of these tools can feel more inclined to use them in their future works because of their increased understandings of the strategies' significance. I recently spoke with an eighth-grade student who explained that reflecting on the writing strategies she learned made her more inclined to use them in her other writings: "I liked answering the reflection questions. I think they helped me think about why the things we learned about are good for writing, and made it easier for me to use those things when I wrote other stories."

Recommendation Six: Facilitate Connections to New Literacies with Your Students

When teaching your students about the tools of narrative writing, I recommend helping them make connections between these writing strategies and technology-focused new literacies. There are a number of ways that multimedia connections can enhance students' abilities to create narratives: Chapters 1–8 of this book contain "New Literacy Connection" sections, which provide examples of how my students and I have linked multimedia with our study of particular writing tools. When connecting new literacies with writing instruction, remember to keep your pedagogical goals in mind: the best technology-infused instruction uses technological aspects strategically, with clear understandings of how each aspect of multimedia can improve students' learning. Chapter 4 of this book, which focuses on incorporating characterization, contains a strong example of connecting multimedia with narrative writing: that chapter's "New Literacy Connection" discusses a student who used audio files of music to help readers understand her story's protagonist. This character is greatly impacted by the music of the rapper 2Pac, so the student decided to include links to 2Pac's music to enhance readers' experiences and understanding. Specific methods of incorporating multimedia into narrative writing can vary, based on the writing strategy being discussed, as well as students' and teachers' levels of familiarity with different technological components. The examples in this book can help you create these new literacy connections with your students!

Recommendation Seven: Show Students How Narrative Writing Tools Are Present in a Range of Content Areas

Narrative-writing tools are not just for fictional pieces composed in English class; students can apply these writing strategies to a number of content areas. Some of the student writing samples featured in this book represent this possibility: Chapter 5 includes an excerpt from a narrative a student wrote about Paul Revere for his social studies class; in this narrative, the student incorporated the narrative-writing tool of using transitional language to create a sense of cohesion in his piece. Another example of a content-area narrative featured in this book is a student's piece about solar eclipses described in Chapter 6; in this work, the student author used the strategy of including concrete language to explain the steps of a solar eclipse as clearly and concretely as possible. The concrete language this student uses—strong verbs such as "blotted out," and specific nouns like "orbit"—make the narrative engaging, while also revealing his understanding of this natural occurrence. Through the use of the narrative-writing tools described in this book, students can make their content-area writings enjoyable to read, while also conveying their knowledge as clearly and effectively as possible.

Final Thoughts on the Narrative Writing Toolkit

I recently tutored a sixth-grade basketball player who had been struggling with writing. In our first meeting, I used his interest in basketball to build a bridge to mentor texts: "What do you pay attention to when you watch a basketball game?" I asked him.

"A lot of things," he replied. "It's not just who's winning. I look at what the players are doing, like what moves they're using on the defenders."

"Do you then imitate what those players do when you play?" I followed up.

"Yeah, totally. Like, I'll watch a move that a player on TV will use and then I'll try it out in my driveway or at practice."

"Fantastic!" I responded, thrilled that his comments set up a perfect connection to mentor-text-based writing instruction. "That's exactly the kind of thing we're going to do when we talk about writing. We're going to look at published narratives, talk about what tactics the authors of those narratives use, and then you're going to try using them in your own writing, just like basketball. Sound good?"

"Yeah, sounds good," he beamed, confidently scooting his chair up to the table where we were working.

This anecdote captures the power and relevance of mentor-text-based writing instruction; just as students emulate experts in other areas, we teachers can help take this same apprenticeship framework to their narrative writing. Perhaps the thing I most love about using mentor texts to teach the writing strategies described in this book is that I never feel alone: I have countless published narratives from which I can draw as I identify and explain the important elements. This book provides many resources and ideas for you to use as you do the same!

Section **3**

Resources

Appendix A
Reproducible Charts and Forms You Can Use in Your Classroom

This appendix contains reproducible versions of key charts and forms featured in this book. It is designed to help you put the ideas in this book into action in your classroom!

Table A1 Table Graphic Organizer for Student Analysis of Text Openings

Text Meant to Engage Readers	How Can You Tell This Text Is Meant to Engage Readers?	Text Meant to Orient Readers	How Can You Tell This Text Is Meant to Orient Readers?

© 2016, *The Narrative Writing Toolkit*, Sean Ruday, Taylor & Francis

Table A2 Graphic Organizer for Event Sequence Activity

Aspects of Narrative Sequence	Corresponding Quotations from Text
Exposition	
Rising Action	
Climax	
Falling Action	
Resolution	

Reflection question: Why is it important that the text you used followed this narrative sequence?

© 2016, *The Narrative Writing Toolkit*, Sean Ruday, Taylor & Francis

Table A3 Event Description Analysis Handout

Original, Detailed Description of an Important Event in Your Book	Revised, Concise Version of This Event Description	Why You Think the Author Chose to Write a Detailed Description of the Event

© 2016, *The Narrative Writing Toolkit*, Sean Ruday, Taylor & Francis

Table A4 Characterization Analysis Chart

Characterization Passage that "Shows"	Passage Revised to "Tell" instead of "Show"	Why it's Important that the Original Passage "Shows" instead of "Tells"

© 2016, *The Narrative Writing Toolkit*, Sean Ruday, Taylor & Francis

Table A5 Template for Comparison of Published Text with and without Transitional Language

Original Text	Text without Transitional Language	Why the Transitional Language Is Important to the Original Passage

© 2016, *The Narrative Writing Toolkit*, Sean Ruday, Taylor & Francis

Table A6 Graphic Organizer for Concrete Language Analysis (Blank Version of Table 6.3)

Published Sentence that uses Concrete Language	Concrete Language in Sentence	Revised Version with General Language Instead of Concrete Language	Your Analysis of the Difference in the Sentences

© 2016, *The Narrative Writing Toolkit*, Sean Ruday, Taylor & Francis

Table A7 Graphic Organizer for Sensory Detail Analysis (Blank Version of Table 7.3)

Original Passage	Revised Version with Sensory Details Omitted	Why the Sensory Details Are Important to the Original Passage

© 2016, *The Narrative Writing Toolkit*, Sean Ruday, Taylor & Francis

Table A8 Graphic Organizer for Conclusion Analysis (Blank Version of Table 8.2)

Conclusion	How it Provides a Sense of Closure	How it Provides a Final Message	Why it Is Important to the Effectiveness of the Narrative

© 2016, *The Narrative Writing Toolkit*, Sean Ruday, Taylor & Francis

Table A9 Evaluation Criteria for Engaging and Orienting the Reader

Writing Tool	Evaluation Criteria	Possible Points	Your Score
Engaging and orienting the reader	◆ Does the piece's introductory text capture the readers' interest and encourage them to continue with the narrative? ◆ Does the opening section begin to introduce key information about the narrative, such as who the main characters are, where the story takes place, and what takes place?	4	

Comments:

© 2016, *The Narrative Writing Toolkit*, Sean Ruday, Taylor & Francis

Table A10 Evaluation Criteria for Organizing an Event Sequence

Writing Tool	Evaluation Criteria	Possible Points	Your Score
Organizing an event sequence	♦ Does the piece contain all of the aspects of narrative sequence (exposition, rising action, climax, falling action, and resolution)? ♦ Are the aspects of narrative sequence presented in order? ♦ Can the aspects of narrative sequence be clearly determined?	4	

Comments:

© 2016, *The Narrative Writing Toolkit*, Sean Ruday, Taylor & Francis

Table A11 Evaluation Criteria for Developing Experiences and Events

Writing Tool	Evaluation Criteria	Possible Points	Your Score
Developing experiences and events	♦ Does the narrative describe experiences and events in detail, using components such as the event's setting, a character's actions, a character's motivation, a conversation between characters, and a character's thoughts? ♦ Are the experiences and events described significant to the narrative? ♦ Do these descriptions communicate the importance of these experiences and events?	4	

Comments:

© 2016, *The Narrative Writing Toolkit*, Sean Ruday, Taylor & Francis

Table A12 Evaluation Criteria for Incorporating Characterization

Writing Tool	Evaluation Criteria	Possible Points	Your Score
Incorporating characterization	◆ Does the narrative include important information about characters that helps readers understand them? ◆ Does the narrative convey information about characters through behaviors such as actions, thoughts, and dialogue, and allow readers to infer those characteristics?	4	

Comments:

© 2016, *The Narrative Writing Toolkit*, Sean Ruday, Taylor & Francis

Table A13 Evaluation Criteria for Including Transitional Language

Writing Tool	Evaluation Criteria	Possible Points	Your Score
Including transitional language	♦ Does the narrative contain transitional language that establishes relationships between events and ideas? ♦ Does the transitional language communicate clearly and accurately how ideas and events in the narrative relate to each other?	4	

Comments:

© 2016, *The Narrative Writing Toolkit*, Sean Ruday, Taylor & Francis

Table A14 Evaluation Criteria for Using Concrete Words and Phrases

Writing Tool	Evaluation Criteria	Possible Points	Your Score
Using concrete words and phrases	♦ Does the narrative contain examples of concrete language, such as specific nouns and strong verbs? ♦ Do these examples of concrete language express specific information clearly? ♦ Does the specific information expressed by the concrete language examples make sense in the context of the narrative?	4	

Comments:

© 2016, *The Narrative Writing Toolkit*, Sean Ruday, Taylor & Francis

Table A15 Evaluation Criteria for Creating Sensory Details

Writing Tool	Evaluation Criteria	Possible Points	Your Score
Creating sensory details	♦ Does the piece contain details that appeal to the reader's senses? ♦ Do these sensory details highlight information that is especially important to the event or image being described?	4	

Comments:

© 2016, *The Narrative Writing Toolkit*, Sean Ruday, Taylor & Francis

Table A16 Evaluation Criteria for Crafting a Strong Conclusion

Writing Tool	Evaluation Criteria	Possible Points	Your Score
Crafting a strong conclusion	♦ Does the conclusion provide readers with a sense of closure to the story's events? ♦ Does the conclusion leave readers with a final message related to those events?	4	

Comments:

© 2016, *The Narrative Writing Toolkit*, Sean Ruday, Taylor & Francis

Appendix B
A Guide for Book Studies

The Narrative Writing Toolkit is ideally suited for groups of elementary and middle-school teachers who are interested in teaching their students the key components of narrative writing in engaging and effective ways, and who want to work together as a book-study group. If you are using this text for a book study, I recommend you and your group members reflect on important issues in the book at three distinct stages: before reading; during reading; and after reading. The sections discussed below provide key points to consider before examining the text, while you're reading it, and once you've completed it.

Before Reading

Before reading this text, I suggest activating your prior knowledge of this book's central points by considering three key ideas:

- What are some narratives (written at your students' reading levels) that strike you as especially strong?
- What writing strategies do you feel these authors use to make their works so effective?
- How might you help your students include these strategies in their own writings?

During Reading

I recommend answering the four questions below with your book group members at the conclusion of each chapter between Chapter 1 and Chapter 8:

- What makes the narrative writing strategy described in this chapter important to effective writing?
- Which of the mentor texts described in this chapter do you think could be used most effectively with your students?
- How might you apply ideas from this chapter's "New Literacy Connection" to your instruction?
- What are some questions you'd ask your students as they work on including this chapter's focal strategy in their own writing?

© 2016, *The Narrative Writing Toolkit*, Sean Ruday, Taylor & Francis

Next, read Chapter 9 and discuss the following questions with the other members of your book-study group:

- What are some benefits that can come from separately evaluating each aspect of effective narrative writing?
- This chapter addresses differentiation by explaining that students can be evaluated on specific writing tools that represent what they are able to do at that time. How might you apply this method of differentiation to your classroom?

After reading Chapter 9 and answering the above questions, read Chapter 10 and discuss the following with your group members:

- How do you feel the ideas discussed in Chapter 10 work together to create strong narrative-writing instruction?

After Reading

Now that you've finished *The Narrative Writing Toolkit*, talk with your book-study group about your responses to these four questions:

- How did the ideas in this book enhance your understanding of how to use mentor texts in narrative-writing instruction?
- Which of the narrative-writing tools described in this book do you see as most important for effective narrative writing?
- Reflection is a major part of this book—students reflect on the importance of each writing tool after using it in their works. How will you help your students reflect on the writing strategies you teach them?
- What is one way you feel this book will immediately impact your writing instruction?

© 2016, *The Narrative Writing Toolkit*, Sean Ruday, Taylor & Francis

Annotated Bibliography
Excerpts from Published Works Featured in This Book, Aligned with Specific Common Core Standards

This annotated bibliography contains the following information:

1. The titles and authors of the published texts that I describe in this book as exemplars of the tools of effective narrative writing.
2. A tool of effective narrative writing found in each work.
3. The Common Core State Writing Standards associated with that tool.
4. An excerpt from that work, found earlier in this book, that demonstrates exactly how the author uses that narrative writing tool.
5. Information on which chapter in this book the concept is discussed (in case you want to refer back to the text for more information on a concept).

The annotated bibliography is designed to make this book as user-friendly as possible. It is organized alphabetically by author's last name, and each entry includes important details designed to help you use these published works to teach your students about the tools of narrative writing.

Arnosky, J. (2009). *The Pirates of Crocodile Swamp.* New York, NY: G.P. Putnam's Sons.
Title: *The Pirates of Crocodile Swamp*
Author: Jim Arnosky
Narrative Writing Tool: Creating sensory details
Related Common Core State Standards: W.4.3.D, W.5.3.D, W.6.3.D, W.7.3.D, W.8.3.D
Excerpts that Demonstrate Concept:

"Jack set up our tiny stove on the beach and heated our frying pan full of salt water to cook the crabs he had caught earlier. When the water was boiling, I plopped in the crabs. After a few minutes, their blue shells turned bright red, and we had fresh crabmeat for lunch. Being cooked in salt water made the meat extra salty, but we didn't mind. It tasted good to us." (p. 92)

"'Ugh!' he said. 'Sandy, hold my nose. This stinks!'
I held Jack's nose and my own. Jack chopped off the fish's head and peeled off its scaly skin." (p. 93)

Discussed in Chapter: 7

© 2016, *The Narrative Writing Toolkit*, Sean Ruday, Taylor & Francis

Auch, M.J. (1998). *I was a Third Grade Science Project*. New York, NY: Holiday House.
Title: *I was a Third Grade Science Project*
Author: Mary Jane Auch
Narrative Writing Tool: Engaging and orienting the reader
Related Common Core State Standards: W.3.3.A, W.4.3.A, W.5.3.A, W.6.3.A, W.7.3.A, W.8.3.A
Excerpt that Demonstrates Concept:

"Having a genius for a friend can be real trouble." (p. 1)

Discussed in Chapter: 1

Boyce, F.C. (2004). *Millions*. New York, NY: HarperCollins.
Title: *Millions*
Author: Frank Cottrell Boyce
Narrative Writing Tool: Including transitional language
Related Common Core State Standards: W.3.3.C, W.4.3.C, W.5.3.C, W.6.3.C, W.7.3.C, W.8.3.C
Excerpts that Demonstrate Concept:

"Mr. Quinn came over and touched my shoulder. Then he leaned down and whispered to me to come with him." (p. 21)

"If Anthony was telling this story, he'd start with the money. It always comes down to money, he says, so you might as well start there. He'd probably put, 'Once upon a time there were 229,370 little pounds sterling,' and go on until he got to, 'and they all lived happily ever after in a high-interest bank account.' But he's not telling this story. I am." (p. 1)

Discussed in Chapter: 5

Brashares, A. (2001). *The Sisterhood of the Traveling Pants*. New York, NY: Delacorte Press.
Title: *The Sisterhood of the Traveling Pants*
Author: Ann Brashares
Narrative Writing Tool: Using concrete words and phrases
Related Common Core State Standards: W.4.3.D, W.5.3.D, W.6.3.D, W.7.3.D, W.8.3.D
Excerpt that Demonstrates Concept:

"Sweat dripped down from her thick, dark hair onto her neck and temples." (p. 107)

© 2016, *The Narrative Writing Toolkit*, Sean Ruday, Taylor & Francis

Discussed in Chapter: 6

Cormier, R. (1974). *The Chocolate War.* New York, NY: Bantam.
Title: *The Chocolate War*
Author: Robert Cormier
Narrative Writing Tool: Using concrete words and phrases
Related Common Core State Standards: W.4.3.D, W.5.3.D, W.6.3.D, W.7.3.D, W.8.3.D
Excerpt that Demonstrates Concept:

"'I've got guts,' Jerry murmured, getting up by degrees, careful not to displace any of his bones or sinews." (p. 7)

Discussed in Chapter: 6

Coville, B. (1992). *My Teacher Flunked the Planet.* New York, NY: Minstrel Books.
Title: *My Teacher Flunked the Planet*
Author: Bruce Coville
Narrative Writing Tool: Including transitional language
Related Common Core State Standards: W.3.3.C, W.4.3.C, W.5.3.C, W.6.3.C, W.7.3.C, W.8.3.C
Excerpt that Demonstrates Concept:

"As the end of the mission drew closer, the dreams got worse. Also Susan and I noticed something strange . . ." (p. 95)

Discussed in Chapter: 5

Creech, S. (1996). *Pleasing the Ghost.* New York, NY: Scholastic.
Title: *Pleasing the Ghost*
Author: Sharon Creech
Narrative Writing Tool: Incorporating characterization
Related Common Core State Standards: W.3.3.B, W.4.3.B, W.5.3.B, W.6.3.B, W.7.3.B, W.8.3.B
Excerpt that Demonstrates Concept:

"Bo bounded down the stairs, out the door, and stopped at the curb, wagging his tail. I led him across the street, and he leaped toward Uncle Arvie, barking and wiggling his back end. He tumbled right through Uncle Arvie and collapsed on the ground. 'Yip!' he squeaked." (p. 18)

© 2016, *The Narrative Writing Toolkit*, Sean Ruday, Taylor & Francis

Discussed in Chapter: 4

Dahl, R. (1980). *The Twits*. New York, NY: Puffin Books.
Title: *The Twits*
Author: Roald Dahl
Narrative Writing Tool: Developing experiences and events
Related Common Core State Standards: W.3.3.B, W.4.3.B, W.5.3.B, W.6.3.B, W.7.3.B, W.8.3.B
Excerpt that Demonstrates Concept:

"When that was done, he began filling the balloons with gas. Each balloon was on a long string and when it was filled with gas it pulled on its string, trying to go up and up. Mr. Twit tied the ends of the strings to the top half of Mrs. Twit's body. Some he tied around her neck, some under her arms, some to her wrists and some even to her hair." (p. 24)

Discussed in Chapter: 3

DiCamillo, K. (2003). *The tale of Despereaux*. Somerville, MA: Candlewick Press.
Title: *The Tale of Despereaux*
Author: Kate DiCamillo
Narrative Writing Tool: Engaging and orienting the reader
Related Common Core State Standards: W.3.3.A, W.4.3.A, W.5.3.A, W.6.3.A, W.7.3.A, W.8.3.A
Excerpt that Demonstrates Concept:

"This story begins within the walls of a castle, with the birth of a mouse. A small mouse. The last mouse born to his parents and the only one of his litter to be born alive.
 'Where are my babies?' said the exhausted mother when the ordeal was through. 'Show to me my babies.'
 The father mouse held the one small mouse up high.
 'There is only this one,' he said. 'The others are dead.'" (p. 11)

Discussed in Chapter: 1

Fleischman, P. (1997). *Seedfolks*. New York, NY: Harper Trophy.
Title: *Seedfolks*
Author: Paul Fleischman
Narrative Writing Tool: Crafting a strong conclusion

© 2016, *The Narrative Writing Toolkit*, Sean Ruday, Taylor & Francis

Related Common Core State Standards: W.3.3.E, W.4.3.E, W.5.3.E, W.6.3.E, W.7.3.E, W.8.3.E
Excerpts that Demonstrate Concept:

"My class had sprouted lima beans in paper cups the year before. I now placed a bean in each of the holes. I covered them up, pressing the soil down firmly with my fingertips. I opened my thermos and watered them all. And I vowed to myself that those beans would thrive." (p. 4)

"He showed me exactly how far apart the rows should be and how deep. He couldn't read the words on the seed packet, but he knew from the pictures what seeds were inside. He poured them into his hand and smiled. He seemed to recognize them, like old friends. Watching him carefully sprinkling them into the troughs he made, I realized that I didn't know anything about growing food and that he knew everything. I stared at his busy fingers, then his eyes. They were focused, not far-away or confused. He changed from a baby back into a man." (p. 22)

Discussed in Chapter: 8

Gannett, R.S. (1950). *Elmer and the Dragon.* New York, NY: Yearling.
Title: *Elmer and the Dragon*
Author: Ruth Stiles Gannett
Narrative Writing Tool: Engaging and orienting the reader
Related Common Core State Standards: W.3.3.A, W.4.3.A, W.5.3.A, W.6.3.A, W.7.3.A, W.8.3.A
Excerpt that Demonstrates Concept:

"Into the evening sky flew Elmer Elevator aboard the gentle baby dragon, leaving Wild Island behind forever. Elmer, who was nine years old, had just rescued the dragon from the ferocious animals who lived on the island. An old alley cat told him how the dragon had been hurt when he fell from a cloud onto the island, and how the wild animals had made him their miserable prisoner. Elmer, feeling sorry for the dragon, and also hoping to fly on his back, had set off to the rescue." (p. 1)

Discussed in Chapter: 1

Gantos, J. (2007). *I am Not Joey Pigza.* New York, NY: Farrar, Strauss, and Giroux.
Title: *I am Not Joey Pigza*

© 2016, *The Narrative Writing Toolkit*, Sean Ruday, Taylor & Francis

Author: Jack Gantos
Narrative Writing Tool: Incorporating characterization
Related Common Core State Standards: W.3.3.B, W.4.3.B, W.5.3.B, W.6.3.B, W.7.3.B, W.8.3.B
Excerpt that Demonstrates Concept:

"And then he stood on a chair and gave an amazing speech about how Mom was the greatest woman in the world, with the most forgiving heart and the most angelic face, and that he was the luckiest man on the planet." (p. 51)

Discussed in Chapter: 4

Grabenstein, C. (2013). *Escape from Mr. Lemoncello's Library*. New York, NY: Random House.
Author: Chris Grabenstein
Title: *Escape from Mr. Lemoncello's Library*
Narrative Writing Tool: Including transitional language
Related Common Core State Standards: W.3.3.C, W.4.3.C, W.5.3.C, W.6.3.C, W.7.3.C, W.8.3.C
Excerpt that Demonstrates Concept:

"For this assembly, the seventh graders, most of whom were twelve years old, were told to sit in the front rows, close to the stage. That made Kyle feel a little better. At least he'd get a chance to see Mr. Lemoncello up close and personal. But his hero wasn't even onstage." (p. 32f)

Discussed in Chapter: 5

Grisham, J. (2011). *Theodore Boone: The Abduction*. New York, NY: Dutton Children's Books.
Title: *Theodore Boone: The Abduction*
Author: John Grisham
Narrative Writing Tool: Using concrete words and phrases
Related Common Core State Standards: W.4.3.D, W.5.3.D, W.6.3.D, W.7.3.D, W.8.3.D
Excerpt that Demonstrates Concept:

"In the hall, he whipped out his cell phone and called Ike." (p. 107)

Discussed in Chapter: 6

© 2016, *The Narrative Writing Toolkit*, Sean Ruday, Taylor & Francis

Hawthorne, W. (2009). *The Last Pirate.* Cape Coral, FL: Eyeland Telemedia.
Title: *The Last Pirate*
Author: Wilson Hawthorne
Narrative Writing Tool: Creating sensory details
Related Common Core State Standards: W.4.3.D, W.5.3.D, W.6.3.D, W.7.3.D, W.8.3.D
Excerpt that Demonstrates Concept:

"I kept looking over the charts until, after a while, it started to rain. Nothing put me to sleep quicker than the sound of rain hitting the metal roof of our mobile home. My eyes got tired first. I looked over at Hammerhead. He was already snoring. I put everything away on top of the dresser and turned off the light. My room wasn't dark, though. The streetlight outside the window takes care of that. I could read by it if I wanted to." (p. 55)

Discussed in Chapter: 7

Another Narrative Writing Tool Found in This Book: Crafting a strong conclusion
Related Common Core State Standards: W.3.3.E, W.4.3.E, W.5.3.E, W.6.3.E, W.7.3.E, W.8.3.E
Excerpt that Demonstrates Concept:

"She slugged me in the arm. 'You don't even have a watch,' she laughed.
'Well, neither do you.'
'Know what else you don't have?'
'What's that?'
'A first mate,' she said.
'You looking for a job?'
'More like a partnership.'
'Seal it with a kiss?'
The tide carried us out to sea.
Life is a roller coaster, right? Hang on and enjoy the ride. And write some history you'd let anybody read. That's my advice.
At that moment, I was hanging on with both arms and all my heart. And out on the sea next to his island, I finally understood what turned that old pirate around.
Some diddie, huh?" (p. 213)

Discussed in Chapter: 8

© 2016, *The Narrative Writing Toolkit*, Sean Ruday, Taylor & Francis

Hiaasen, C. (2005). *Flush.* New York, NY: Alfred A. Knopf.
Title: *Flush*
Author: Carl Hiaasen
Narrative Writing Tool: Incorporating characterization
Related Common Core State Standards: W.3.3.B, W.4.3.B, W.5.3.B, W.6.3.B, W.7.3.B, W.8.3.B
Excerpt that Demonstrates Concept:

"But Jasper Jr. didn't hit me again. Instead he spit in my face, which was worse in a way.
     He forced a laugh and called me a couple of dirty names and headed back toward the johnboat. He was shaking that hand he'd hit me with, as if there was a crab or a mousetrap attached to it. Bull was following behind, cackling like a hyena." (p. 38)

Discussed in Chapter: 4

Juster, N. (1961). *The Phantom Tollbooth.* New York, NY: Random House.
Title: *The Phantom Tollbooth*
Author: Norton Juster
Narrative Writing Tool: Developing experiences and events
Related Common Core State Standards: W.3.3.B, W.4.3.B, W.5.3.B, W.6.3.B, W.7.3.B, W.8.3.B
Excerpt that Demonstrates Concept:

"Without stopping or looking up, Milo dashed past the buildings and busy shops that lined the street and in a few minutes reached home—dashed through the lobby—hopped onto the elevator—two, three, four, five, six, seven, eight, and off again—opened the apartment door—rushed into his room—flopped dejectedly into a chair, and grumbled softly, 'Another long afternoon.'" (p. 11)

Discussed in Chapter: 3

Kehret, P. (2004). *Abduction!* New York, NY: Dutton Children's Books.
Title: *Abduction!*
Author: Peg Kehret
Narrative Writing Tool: Using concrete words and phrases
Related Common Core State Standards: W.4.3.D, W.5.3.D, W.6.3.D, W.7.3.D, W.8.3.D
Excerpt that Demonstrates Concept:

"Matt stared out the car window, fighting nausea." (p. 62)

Discussed in Chapter: 6

© 2016, *The Narrative Writing Toolkit*, Sean Ruday, Taylor & Francis

Konigsburg, E.L. (1967). *From the Mixed-Up Files of Mrs. Basil E. Frankweiler.* New York, NY: Atheneum Books for Young Readers.
Title: *From the Mixed-Up Files of Mrs. Basil E. Frankweiler*
Author: E.L. Konigsburg
Narrative Writing Tool: Incorporating characterization
Related Common Core State Standards: W.3.3.B, W.4.3.B, W.5.3.B, W.6.3.B, W.7.3.B, W.8.3.B
Excerpt that Demonstrates Concept:

"Claudia knew that she could never pull off the old-fashioned kind of running away. That is, running away in the heat of anger with a knapsack on her back. She didn't like discomfort; even picnics were untidy and inconvenient: all those insects and the sun melting the ice on the cupcakes. Therefore, she decided that her leaving home would not be just running from somewhere but would be running to somewhere. To a large place, a comfortable place, an indoor place, and preferably a beautiful place. And that's why she decided upon the Metropolitan Museum of Art in New York City." (p. 5)

Discussed in Chapter: 4

Kinney, J. (2013). *Diary of a Wimpy Kid: Hard Luck.* New York, NY: Amulet Books.
Title: *Diary of Wimpy Kid: Hard Luck*
Author: Jeff Kinney
Narrative Writing Tool: Incorporating characterization
Related Common Core State Standards: W.3.3.B, W.4.3.B, W.5.3.B, W.6.3.B, W.7.3.B, W.8.3.B
Excerpt that Demonstrates Concept:

"Wherever Rowley is, his girlfriend Abigail is, too. And even if she ISN'T there, it SEEMS like she is. I invited Rowley to my house for a sleepover last weekend so the two of us could spend some time together, but after about two hours I gave up trying to have any fun." (p. 4)

Discussed in Chapter: 4

Lupica, M. (2009). *Million Dollar Throw.* New York, NY: Philomel Books.
Title: *Million Dollar Throw*
Author: Mike Lupica
Narrative Writing Tool: Creating sensory details
Related Common Core State Standards: W.4.3.D, W.5.3.D, W.6.3.D, W.7.3.D, W.8.3.D

© 2016, *The Narrative Writing Toolkit*, Sean Ruday, Taylor & Francis

Excerpt that Demonstrates Concept:

"This was always the best of it for Nate Brodie, when he felt the slap of the ball in his hands and began to back away from the center, when he felt as if he could see the whole field, and football made perfect sense to him." (p. 1)

Discussed in Chapter: 7

Osborne, M.P. (1995). *Night of the Ninjas.* New York, NY: Random House.
Title: *Night of the Ninjas*
Author: Mary Pope Osborne
Narrative Writing Tool: Organizing an event sequence
Related Common Core State Standards: W.3.3.A, W.4.3.A, W.5.3.A, W.6.3.A, W.7.3.A, W.8.3.A
Excerpts that Demonstrate Concept:

Exposition:
"The magic tree house was back.
'Come on up!' Annie shouted.
Jack ran to the rope ladder. He started climbing." (p. 5)

Rising Action:
"Jack peeked over the windowsill. His eyes met the dark eyes of the tall ninja." (p. 16)

Climax:
"Jack and Annie crouched together. Samurai were on both sides of them now. They were trapped!" (p. 48)

Falling Action:
"'You have done well,' the figure said.
It was the ninja master.
'You have followed the way of the ninja,' he said." (p. 59)

Resolution:
"Together they took off through the cool, dark woods.
They moved silently and swiftly—two shadow warriors returning home." (p. 69)

Discussed in Chapter: 2

© 2016, *The Narrative Writing Toolkit*, Sean Ruday, Taylor & Francis

Paulsen, G. (1985). *Dogsong*. New York, NY: Aladdin Paperbacks.
Title: *Dogsong*
Author: Gary Paulsen
Narrative Writing Tool: Creating sensory details
Related Common Core State Standards: W.4.3.D, W.5.3.D, W.6.3.D, W.7.3.D, W.8.3.D
Excerpt that Demonstrates Concept:

"The frozen seal meat started to melt and give off oil immediately and the caribou began to cook in the oil and soon the smell of the meat filled the room and he liked that." (p. 8)

Discussed in Chapter: 7

Rockwell, T. (1973). *How to Eat Fried Worms*. New York, NY: Bantam Doubleday Dell.
Title: *How to Eat Fried Worms*
Author: Thomas Rockwell
Narrative Writing Tool: Developing experiences and events
Related Common Core State Standards: W.3.3.B, W.4.3.B, W.5.3.B, W.6.3.B, W.7.3.B, W.8.3.B
Excerpt that Demonstrates Concept:

"So Tom took Billy aside into a horse stall and put his arm around Billy's shoulder and talked to him about George Cunningham's brother's minibike, and how they could ride it on the trail under the power lines behind Odell's farm, up and down the hills, bounding over rocks, rhum-rhum. Sure it was a big worm, but it'd only be a couple more bites. Did he want to lose a minibike over *two bites*? Slop enough mustard and ketchup and horseradish on it and he wouldn't even taste it." (p. 15)

Discussed in Chapter: 3

Sachar, L. (1975). *Sideways Stories from Wayside School*. New York, NY: HarperCollins.
Title: *Sideways Stories from Wayside School*
Author: Louis Sachar
Narrative Writing Tool: Organizing an event sequence
Related Common Core State Standards: W.3.3.A, W.4.3.A, W.5.3.A, W.6.3.A, W.7.3.A, W.8.3.A
Excerpts that Demonstrate Concept:

© 2016, *The Narrative Writing Toolkit*, Sean Ruday, Taylor & Francis

Exposition:
"Mrs. Gorf had a long tongue and pointed ears. She was the meanest teacher in Wayside School." (p. 11)

Rising Action:
"She wiggled her ears—first her right one, then her left—stuck out her tongue, and turned Joe into an apple." (p. 12)

Climax:
"Mrs. Gorf fell on the floor. The apples jumped all over her." (p. 14)

Falling Action:
"She stuck out her tongue, wiggled her ears—this time her left one first, then her right—and turned the apples back into children." (p. 14)

Resolution:
"But Jenny held up a mirror, and Mrs. Gorf turned herself into an apple . . . He picked up the apple, which was really Mrs. Gorf, shined it up on his shirt, and ate it." (p. 14)

Discussed in Chapter: 2

Sheth, K. (2004). *Blue Jasmine*. New York, NY: Hyperion.
Title: *Blue Jasmine*
Author: Kashmira Sheth
Narrative Writing Tool: Incorporating characterization
Related Common Core State Standards: W.3.3.B, W.4.3.B, W.5.3.B, W.6.3.B, W.7.3.B, W.8.3.B
Excerpt that Demonstrates Concept:

"I got up. My hand was shaking as I wrote on the blackboard. Between me and the blackboard was my warm breath, which made me break out in a sweat." (p. 52)

Discussed in Chapter: 4

Snicket, L. (1999). *The Bad Beginning*. New York, NY: HarperCollins.
Title: *The Bad Beginning*
Author: Lemony Snicket
Narrative Writing Tool: Engaging and orienting the reader
Related Common Core State Standards: W.3.3.A, W.4.3.A, W.5.3.A, W.6.3.A, W.7.3.A, W.8.3.A
Excerpt that Demonstrates Concept:

"If you are interested in stories with happy endings, you would be better off reading some other book. In this book, not only is there no happy ending, there is no happy beginning and very few happy things happen in the middle. This is because not very many happy things happened in the lives of the three Baudelaire youngsters. Violet, Klaus, and Sunny Baudelaire were intelligent children, and they were charming, and resourceful, and had pleasant facial features, but they were extremely unlucky, and most everything that happened to them was rife with misfortunate, misery, and despair." (p. 1)

Discussed in Chapter: 1

Snicket, L. (2013). *When Did You See Her Last?* New York, NY: Little, Brown, and Company.
Title: *When Did You See Her Last?*
Author: Lemony Snicket
Narrative Writing Tool: Using concrete words and phrases
Related Common Core State Standards: W.4.3.D, W.5.3.D, W.6.3.D, W.7.3.D, W.8.3.D
Excerpt that Demonstrates Concept:

"I slipped the needle out of the tire." (p. 55)

Discussed in Chapter: 6

Spinelli, J. (1990). *Maniac Magee.* Boston, MA: Little, Brown, and Company.
Title: *Maniac Magee*
Author: Jerry Spinelli
Narrative Writing Tool: Creating sensory details
Related Common Core State Standards: W.4.3.D, W.5.3.D, W.6.3.D, W.7.3.D, W.8.3.D
Excerpt that Demonstrates Concept:

"They were members of the town's trash-collecting corps, and as they huffed and bent to lay the box over the hole, they smelled vaguely of pine and rotten fruit." (p. 116)

Discussed in Chapter: Introduction

Another Narrative Writing Tool Found in This Book: Using concrete words and phrases

© 2016, *The Narrative Writing Toolkit*, Sean Ruday, Taylor & Francis

Related Common Core State Standards: W.4.3.D, W.5.3.D, W.6.3.D, W.7.3.D, W.8.3.D
Excerpt that Demonstrates Concept:

"George McNab pulled himself up from the easy chair and shuffled back into the kitchen." (p. 163)

Discussed in Chapter: 6

Another Narrative Writing Tool Found in This Book: Crafting a strong conclusion
Related Common Core State Standards: W.3.3.E, W.4.3.E, W.5.3.E, W.6.3.E, W.7.3.E, W.8.3.E
Excerpt that Demonstrates Concept:

"Maniac said nothing. He was quite content to let Amanda do the talking, for he knew that behind her grumbling was all that he had ever wanted. He knew that finally, truly, at long last, someone was calling him home." (p. 184)

Discussed in Chapter: 8

Vanderpool, C. (2010). *Moon over Manifest*. New York, NY: Delacorte Press.
Title: *Moon over Manifest*
Author: Clare Vanderpool
Narrative Writing Tool: Creating sensory details
Related Common Core State Standards: W.4.3.D, W.5.3.D, W.6.3.D, W.7.3.D, W.8.3.D
Excerpt that Demonstrates Concept:

"Smoothing out the yellowed newspaper for the thousandth time, I scanned the page, hoping to find some bit of news or insight into my daddy." (p. 2)

Discussed in Chapter: 7

White, E.B. (1952). *Charlotte's Web*. New York, NY: HarperCollins.
Title: *Charlotte's Web*
Author: E.B. White
Narrative Writing Tool: Engaging and orienting the reader

© 2016, *The Narrative Writing Toolkit*, Sean Ruday, Taylor & Francis

Related Common Core State Standards: W.3.3.A, W.4.3.A, W.5.3.A, W.6.3.A, W.7.3.A, W.8.3.A

Excerpt that Demonstrates Concept:

"'Where's Papa going with that ax?' said Fern to her mother as they were setting the table for breakfast.

'Out to the hoghouse,' replied Mrs. Arable. 'Some pigs were born last night.'

'I don't see why he needs an ax,' continued Fern, who was only eight.

'Well,' said her mother, 'one of the pigs is a runt. It's very small and weak, and it will never amount to anything. So your father has decided to do away with it.'" (p. 1)

Discussed in Chapter: 1

© 2016, *The Narrative Writing Toolkit*, Sean Ruday, Taylor & Francis

References

Arnosky, J. (2009). *The Pirates of Crocodile Swamp.* New York, NY: G.P. Putnam's Sons.

Auch, M.J. (1998). *I was a Third-Grade Science Project.* New York, NY: Holiday House.

Bogard, J. M., & McMackin, M.C. (2012). Combining traditional and new literacies in a 21st century writing workshop. *The Reading Teacher*, 65(5), 313–323.

Boyce, F.C. (2004). *Millions.* New York, NY: HarperCollins.

Brashares, A. (2001). *The Sisterhood of the Traveling Pants.* New York, NY: Delacorte Press.

Common Core State Standards Initiative. (2010). Common Core State Standards for English Language Arts. Retrieved from: www.corestandards.org/ELA-Literacy.

Cormier, R. (1974). *The Chocolate War.* New York, NY: Bantam.

Coville, B. (1992). *My Teacher Flunked the Planet.* New York, NY: Minstrel Books.

Creech, S. (1996). *Pleasing the Ghost.* New York, NY: Scholastic.

Dahl, R. (1980). *The Twits.* New York, NY: Puffin Books.

Dalton, B. (2012). Multimodal composition and the Common Core State Standards. *The Reading Teacher*, 66(4), 333–339.

DiCamillo, K. (2003). *The Tale of Despereaux.* Somerville, MA: Candlewick Press.

Fleischman, P. (1997). *Seedfolks.* New York, NY: Harper Trophy.

Fletcher, R., & Portalupi, J. (2001). *Writing Workshop: The Essential Guide.* Portsmouth, NH: Heinemann.

Gannett, R.S. (1950). *Elmer and the Dragon.* New York, NY: Yearling.

Gantos, J. (2007). *I am Not Joey Pigza.* New York, NY: Farrar, Strauss, and Giroux.

Grabenstein, C. (2013). *Escape from Mr. Lemoncello's Library.* New York, NY: Random House.

Grisham, J. (2011). *Theodore Boone: The Abduction.* New York, NY: Dutton Children's Books.

Hawthorne, W. (2009). *The Last Pirate.* Cape Coral, FL: Eyeland Telemedia.

Hiaasen, C. (2005). *Flush.* New York, NY: Alfred A. Knopf.

Juster, N. (1961). *The Phantom Tollbooth.* New York, NY: Random House.

Kehret, P. (2004). *Abduction!* New York, NY: Dutton Children's Books.

Killgallon, D., & Killgallon, J. (2013). *Paragraphs for Middle School: A Sentence-Composing Approach.* Portsmouth, NH: Heinemann.

Kinney, J. (2013). *Diary of a Wimpy Kid: Hard Luck*. New York, NY: Amulet Books.

Konigsburg, E.L. (1967). *From the Mixed-up Files of Mrs. Basil E. Frankweiler*. New York, NY: Atheneum Books for Young Readers.

Lupica, M. (2009). *Million Dollar Throw*. New York, NY: Philomel Books.

Montgomery, R. (2013). Narrative writing: The orphan child of the Common Core. *Writers Who Care: A Blog Advocating for Authentic Writing Instruction*. Retrieved from: https://writerswhocare.wordpress.com/2013/09/30/narrative-writing-the-orphan-child-of-the-common-core.

Osborne, M.P. (1995). *Night of the Ninjas*. New York, NY: Random House.

Paulsen, G. (1985). *Dogsong*. New York, NY: Aladdin Paperbacks.

Pearson, P. D., & Gallagher, M. C. (1983). The instruction of reading comprehension. *Contemporary Educational Psychology, 8*, 317–344.

Rockwell, T. (1973). *How to Eat Fried Worms*. New York, NY: Bantam Doubleday Dell.

Sachar, L. (1975). *Sideways Stories from Wayside School*. New York, NY: HarperCollins.

Sheth, K. (2004). *Blue Jasmine*. New York, NY: Hyperion.

Snicket, L. (1999). *The Bad Beginning*. New York, NY: HarperCollins.

Snicket, L. (2013). *When Did You See Her Last?* New York, NY: Little, Brown, and Company.

Spinelli, J. (1990). *Maniac Magee*. Boston, MA: Little, Brown, and Company.

Vanderpool, C. (2010). *Moon over Manifest*. New York, NY: Delacorte Press.

White, E.B. (1952). *Charlotte's Web*. New York, NY: HarperCollins.